THE WILL TO ARISE

THE WILL TO ARISE

Women, Tradition, and the Church in Africa

Edited by
Mercy Amba Oduyoye
and
Musimbi R. A. Kanyoro

ORBIS BOOKS

Maryknoll, New York 10545

Third Printing, August 1997

The Catholic Foreign Mission Society of America (Maryknoll) recruits and trains people for overseas missionary service. Through Orbis Books, Maryknoll aims to foster the international dialogue that is essential to mission. The books published, however, reflect the opinions of their authors and are not meant to represent the official position of the society.

Library of Congress Cataloging-in-Publication Data

The will to arise : women, tradition, and the church in Africa /
  edited by Mercy Amba Oduyoye and Musimbi R.A. Kanyoro.
     p. cm.
  Includes bibliographical references.
  ISBN 0-88344-782-7
    1. Women in Christianity—Africa. Sub-Saharan. 2. Africa, Sub-Saharan—Church history. 3. Church work with women—Africa, Sub-Saharan. I. Oduyoye, Mercy Amba. II. Kanyoro, Rachel Angogo, 1953-
BV639.W7W53 1992
261.8'344'0967—dc20
                                             91-45847
                                                  CIP

Contents

Part 3
AFRICAN WOMEN AND THE CHRISTIAN CHURCH

Foreword

Katie G. Cannon

As a member of the African Diaspora, I attended the first meeting of the Biennial Institutes of African Women in Religion and Culture, a project of the Circle of Concerned African Women Theologians in Accra, Ghana, in September 1989. I experienced the presentation of the essays included in this book as the dialogue between an actual world and a possible world. Each day of our week-of-work focused on what actually does happen in the African religious context and what ideally should happen. Women of the African Diaspora cannot afford to escape from being involved in African women's judgments that are not only cultural but ultimately theological. Our African sisters confront us with relevant facts that open possibilities before us so that we become aware of constrictions that hem us in and of burdens that oppress.

The themes in *The Will To Arise: Women, Tradition, and the Church in Africa* constitute the ground base of contemporary African women's theological scholarship. The theologians who have contributed to this text interact with African religious culture in two ways: by giving literary expression to religious aspirations, and by reformulating African women's intimate life with God in the context of African culture. They argue that African Christianity is dependent on cultic forms that mediate a societal order with a referent beyond itself. At their most creative level, these theologians affirm cultural traditions and criticize their

---

Katie G. Cannon is an associate professor of Christian Ethics at the Episcopal Divinity School in Cambridge, Massachusetts.

failings, in order to lead the reader to new visions that can renew religious life in our various existential contexts.

African women theologians critique old theologies in such a way as to make apparent the marginalization of women in the collective religious consciousness of former African writers. They present a certain fixedness as well as many instances of creative tension within the real-lived situation. When describing aspects of African religious life, women theologians work with specific, traditional materials, composing their arguments in connection with set ritualistic occasions. They present the very nature of the religious act that is part of the homage paid to God and the ancestral spirits. These writers expand the African ritual structures in order to present the ubiquity of the religious motif of hope and transformation.

The majority of these theologians convey the subtleties of Christian folk religion by providing us with examples of pastoral praxis that coexist with oral religious traditions. They retell myths that have evolved slowly within the culture, expressing glimpses of various community understandings of widowhood, polygamy, sexuality, prostitution, and marriage that serve to delineate the faith systems of African Christian culture.

The genius of this work is that each chapter has taken shape in a milieu rich in oral materials and values. In order to make us attentive to a deeper meaning of the world and life, African women theologians have rescued sayings and stories from their ancestral heritage, rendering present the voiceprints of female religious traditions. An indisputable value of this book, *The Will To Arise*, is that African women theologians have turned once-invisible words into reflective, critical insights so that concepts knowable only to sound and hearing are now visible and available to an infinite range of readers.

Introduction

Musimbi R. A. Kanyoro
Mercy Amba Oduyoye

African women theologians have come to realize that as long as men and foreign researchers remain the authorities on culture, rituals, and religion, African women will continue to be spoken of as if they were dead. At the Lambeth Conference of Anglican bishops in 1988, an African woman theologian had the courage to tell the Anglican primates that women had no need nor use for their soliloquies and monologues on subjects such as polygamy, culture, and the authority of the church. Until women's views are listened to and their participation allowed and ensured, the truth will remain hidden, and the call to live the values of the Reign of God will be unheeded.

The Will To Arise is the voice of African women theologians.[1] It is grounded in the challenges of Scripture and results from a new wave of change. African women reading Scripture have begun to see that God's call to them is not passive. It is compelling and compulsory. It is a call to action and it is a call to wholeness that challenges the will and the intellect.

With the exception of Rabiatu Ammah, a Muslim, the women contributing to this anthology are Christian. All of them, Christian and Muslim alike, write about the realities of being African, women, and religious in a continent where religion shapes the life and thinking of the people. They write about controversial elements of life in Africa, such as culture, sexuality, rituals, and rites of passage. These elements of life are part of their religion. Although the Christian church has struggled to replace them

1

with other possibilities that passed for Christian culture, these African elements did not just survive the Christian onslaught — they adamantly resisted being touched. They continued to sprout and to grow like the equatorial weed that is native to the land.

This anthology is divided into three main sections. In her introductory article in Part 1, "Women in African Culture," Mercy Amba Oduyoye, a Ghanaian, writes about West African cultures. She underlines the centrality of religion and ritual and the need to pay particular attention to women's roles other than their biological ones as wives and mothers. She postulates that women's primarily subordinate participation in rituals reflects their roles in society and the church. She maintains the importance of sexuality in understanding personhood and the divinity of God.

Rosemary N. Edet, a Nigerian, focuses on childbirth and the myths, beliefs, and practices associated with it. She develops the theme that although children are loved and celebrated, both sexuality and birthing are viewed negatively within cultural beliefs. She makes a strong link between sexuality and violence, and illustrates it with examples from African oral literature, myths, and rituals.

The tension between African birth and naming rituals is further explored by Anne Nasimiyu-Wasike of Kenya, who links them with Christian rituals of purification and baptism. She sees possibilities of a more positive approach to purification and baptism on the part of the church and calls for dialogue that would bring the two together in a way that would be truly African and Christian.

This challenge of being both African and Christian threads its way through Daisy Nwachuku's essay. Based on her field research with groups from eighteen different cultures in Nigeria, Nwachuku focuses on widowhood rituals as she explores the dilemma of interpreting African culture with a Christian understanding.

In the last essay in this section, Rabiatu Ammah of Ghana reminds Christian women that their Muslim sisters must equally struggle with these issues. Using the example of clothing, she maintains that the Koran, like the Bible, is often blamed for sanctioning certain attitudes and practices to which women are subjected. She argues that while the Koran states that women should dress simply and decently, various cultures and men's indulgences have interpreted and prescribed many regulations for Muslim women. Like her Christian sister, the Muslim woman always faces the dilemma of floating between the requirements of African culture and the requirements of a second culture, in her case the culture of the Muslim Middle East. Rabiatu Ammah also acknowledges that African women are silenced and heavily burdened and therefore need a will to arise.

Part 2, "African Women and Sexual Practices," deals with the sensitive issues of sexuality. We call them sensitive because African culture and the Christian culture as imported into Africa both bear taboos on talk about sexuality.

The question of polygamy is of vital importance to the topic of African culture and sexuality. The essays by Musimbi R. A. Kanyoro, Anne Nasimiyu-Wasike, and Judith Mbula Bahemuka, all Kenyans, contribute to this debate. Kanyoro's essay focuses on polygamy in Scripture, emphasizing how predominantly male-influenced cultures have influenced both translation and interpretation of the Bible. Nasimiyu and Bahemuka describe the practice of polygamy in Africa. All three women argue that men perpetuate polygamy for their own sexual, patriarchal, and material needs. They claim that polygamy is a form of oppression against women and that the church should stand in solidarity with women to reject this form of oppression.

Lloyda Fanusie of Sierra Leone enters into the barely explored field of traditional sexual taboos and relates them to the exegesis of Scripture to demonstrate the subservient role of women. Fanusie rightly warns against the assumption that we already have enough knowledge about rituals and sexual taboos to understand and to interpret them. She upholds that what is "taboo" is intended to remain secret. Neither women nor men are ordinarily free to tell the details of the taboos, for the telling itself is considered to be taboo.

Bernadette Mbuy Beya of Zaire explores women's sexuality from within the bonds of marriage and family and beyond these bonds. Her study of prostitution in Zaire draws attention to women's needs for education, for respect, and for dignity.

Part 3 focuses on African women within the Christian church.

Teresa Hinga, a Kenyan, analyzes how feminist theologians have sought a form of liberation in Jesus Christ. According to Hinga, the majority of African Christian women confess and accept Jesus Christ as the liberator and perceive Jesus as savior, personal friend, healer, and liberator.

Issues of leadership of women within the church are examined by Anne Nachisale Musopole and R. Modupe Owanikin. Musopole, a Malawian, describes traditional roles of women in an African matriarchal society and emphasizes how these leadership roles can contribute to the African church today. Owanikin, a Nigerian, looks closely at women's leadership in both ordained and administrative ministries in churches in her country and calls for the full and equal participation of women. Finally, Teresa Okure, a Nigerian, uses scriptural reflections to image the conditions from which African women must attain "the will to arise."

A common thread running through these essays is the benefit of learning from the first-hand experiences of women. The Bible was written in a culture similar to our African culture, in which male values were predominant and female values were undermined. Like other disadvantaged people, African women doing theology are often linked with other protest theologies that groan with creation itself. Like these people, too, our purpose is to seek, find, examine, and expose the historical and cultural aspects that are the roots of belief systems that continue to dehumanize women. We are also attempting to bring to the attention of the church in Africa the truth about the love of God, who considers all women and men sinners needful of the grace that comes through Jesus Christ. We are only starting our long journey of faith. We will need to think about methodologies and strategies that will help us achieve our purposes. In this anthology we share experiences in our own lives, in our families, and in those of our sisters, aunts, mothers, and grandmothers. We begin to see patterns emerge as African women search for wholeness and transformation of both the African culture and the church. We see patterns in our desire to share experiences, to reflect together on our respective practices, and to analyze historical events. Patterns are also emerging in our desire to understand better the ecclesiastical office, charisma, prophecy, and ministry.

The study of theology is still a rarity for African women. Africa has only a handful of theological institutions and of these, a majority have no facilities for women. Furthermore, the church rarely makes use of its African women who are trained theologians. Many are assigned to work with educational institutions or with para-church organizations. Among the objectives of African women theologians will be to inspire and stimulate more women to take an interest in theology. A majority of worshipers in the churches of Africa are women. A deeper grounding in theology and a better understanding of Scripture will affect the way they worship. As women themselves discover and remove the obstacles in their way, they will create new and joyful patterns of true worship of the God of Truth.

Finally, we must consider the possible consequences of women's perspectives for the church in Africa. There are many possibilities and positive signs. Women can awaken the church in Africa to the fact that biblical history continues in the lives of God's people. By telling the stories of the struggles and experiences of faith of the People of God today, women will be able to show that the same power of God that enabled Hebrew people to preserve their stories of faith lives with us for whom the promise of the Spirit was given and fulfilled at Pentecost.

As women relate their own experiences, the church in Africa will be forced to listen to a people who have until now been denied a voice. The church will not only listen, but will be enriched by talents and gifts that have remained untapped until today.

Women will gain more courage and respect. As they hear each other, East and West and South and North, African women will begin to see their stories as collective and corporate stories of God's people of faith. These experiences will shape themselves into a litany in which the inessentials will gradually be sloughed off and patterns of common triumph, steadfastness, salvation, and liberation will emerge. African women can no longer withstand *The Will To Arise*.

NOTES

1. The papers in this publication represent the first input of the Biennial Institutes of African Women in Religion and Culture, a project

of the Circle of Concerned African Women Theologians. To contribute to the Circle and to inaugurate the Institute, a call was made for a gathering of African women in theology. There was such an enthusiastic response to the convocation that the editors of this anthology could select only a few of the essays contributed.

PART 1

WOMEN
IN
AFRICAN CULTURE

Women and Ritual in Africa

Mercy Amba Oduyoye

Africa is very hospitable. She has played host to both Christianity and Islam, expecting them to be equally tolerant. They have not been so. Because Christianity and Islam both claim to possess unique and superior revelations, they continue to compete for the conversion of adherents of the primal religions of Africa.

The approaches of Christian and Muslim missionaries, and the efforts of Western colonial governments and their successors among followers of African traditional religions, have all been generally ineffective, primarily because most Westerners lack an understanding of the importance of African religion as an integral part of African culture and life. Westerners have been reluctant to accept the pervasiveness and resilience of religious rituals and the hold they have on people's understanding of life. African rituals have an import that is at once psychological, spiritual, political, and social. Africans operate with an integrated world view that assigns a major place to religious factors and beliefs. It is only those who practice these religious rituals

Mercy Amba Oduyoye, a Ghanaian, is Deputy General Secretary of the World Council of Churches. Educated in the universities of Ghana, Legon, and Cambridge, England, she holds a master's degree in Theology with a specialization in Dogmatics.

who can make a judgment about their modification or their use-
fulness. Africans themselves have the ultimate responsibility for
evaluating their use.

By their integrated nature and their pervasiveness, African
religions exhibit a remarkable similarity to the religions of the
indigenous peoples of the Pacific and those of Native Americans.
It is important to point this out because scholars of African
religion often tend to treat African religions as unique. Instead,
the study of African religion through its rituals can provide an
intercultural perspective to illuminate the various religions of
the world.

WOMEN IN AFRICAN RELIGION

The position of women in Africa today—both within the wider
society and within religion—is normally prescribed by what is
deemed to be beneficial to the welfare of the whole community
of women and men. Unfortunately, most of the prescribing tends
to be carried out by male authorities, and the resulting role of
women tends to be circumscribed by an unchanging set of norms
enshrined in a culture that appears to be equally unchanging.

Much has been said to suggest that the participation of
women in African religion is adequate. It has also been suggested that equality as a concept cannot be applied to African
culture, since role differentiations in Africa are clear and are
not meant to be valued hierarchically. Although it is true that
in Africa women are in charge of shrines and cultic centers, it
is also observable that there are more women in the secondary
roles of mediums and cultic dancers than there are women who
serve as high priests of shrines or as healers. Even more obvious
is the fact that more women than men are clients of the divinities
of the cults. In the African-instituted churches[1] women are most
visible in the structures of authority. However, even here traditional taboos still exclude women, including women founders
of the churches, from sacramental roles.

Religion is an area of life that seems to be able to escape
public attention. It is also an area in which individuals may be
intimidated to abdicate responsibility for their own lives and to

place themselves and everybody else "in God's hands." This should not happen. Christian feminists undertaking "God-talk" must work for the liberation of women from an image of God created for women by men. When examining the role of women in religion in Africa—whether speaking of Christianity, Islam, or African traditional religions—we must face two fundamental questions: What responsibilities do women have in the structures of religion? How does religion serve or obstruct women's development?

THE IMPORTANCE OF RITUAL

African religion gives a major role to rites of passage. An individual's path through life is monitored, marked, and celebrated from even before birth to death and thereafter, and the events in the life of a community echo this same cycle. Throughout a person's life several rituals may be celebrated. Starting a new farm, a new business, a journey, a building—each new venture demands a foundational ritual. Rituals include supplication rites for rain, good health, and children. There are also purification rites to expunge negative influences and contaminations that one has acquired in daily interactions with other people, animals, or objects that are taboo. There are thanksgiving rites for harvest, and for other accomplishments and festivals to celebrate significant events of a community. A brief examination of key rituals and festivals can give us insights into how religion informs and shapes women's lives, and to some extent how life shapes religion.

BIRTH

Birth is marked as the passage from the Other Dimension of time and space to this one. Among the Akan of Ghana, all the rituals of this stage apply equally to boys and girls. On the eighth day, infants of both sexes undergo operations with sexual connotations of beauty and potency. Girls may have their ears pierced and boys are circumcised. Though belonging to the

Akan group, the Asante touch neither boys nor girls, as a person deformed in any way is unfit to perform religious rites. Despite changing fashions, some people from traditional ruling families take care to observe this taboo in order not to jeopardize the chances of their progeny to assume traditional rule in the community.

On the eighth day, a ritual separation from the Other Dimension is effected as the baby is introduced to this world and to the human community of which she or he has become a part. A family name is added to the soul name associated with the day and given to the child at the time of birth. Family names are derived from the generation before one's own parents and may be the masculine or feminine version of a grandparent's name. So far, so good.

When the men and women of the community have assembled for the ritual of naming, the father pronounces the name of the child for all to hear. The mother and all other women have no role in selecting the name. The actions of the name-giving ceremony, those of carrying the baby and putting water and wine into its mouth, are performed by the oldest member of the father's family and a woman may participate.[2] When paternity is disputed, the whole ceremony is usually performed by the mother's family.

PUBERTY

The passage from childhood to adulthood is marked by rites that in some cultures include circumcision for either males or females or for both. The central significance of puberty, however, applies to all ethnic groups. When these rites are performed, a young person becomes a member not only of his or her family but also of the whole community, and takes on adult responsibilities and community responsibilities, including that of replenishing the race.

Among the Asante, pregnancy is an abomination if the puberty rites have not been performed, and the prospective mother and father may be banished. Marriage is not a necessary criteria for child-bearing, although in most matrilineal societies the father does have a significant spiritual role.

Throughout most African cultures, puberty rituals are performed for women by women and for men by men. This is the beginning of the bifurcation of African society. The ritual for girls includes fertility rites, while for boys the rites elicit evidence of bravery. Among the Asante, it is significant that one of the euphemisms for a girl's first menstrual period is that "she has killed an elephant." Similarly, a woman who has given birth is described as "one who has returned safely from the battle front." For women, coming face to face with one's own blood is itself an act of bravery and part of what it means to be a human being. Although a man does not have to kill a lion to be biologically male, some societies require this or some comparable achievement before a man is admitted to the rank of "husband."

MARRIAGE

With marriage a young person's majority is fully recognized, and the individual publicly accepts the responsibility of child-bearing and rearing. The marriage ritual is one of bonding—the physical bonding of two individuals as sexual partners and the covenantal bonding of two families. Performance of the ritual, however, emphasizes the transfer of the woman from the spiritual power of the father to that of the husband. The Yoruba perform a ritual of crossing-over with a washing of feet at the threshold of the husband's house. This element of purification is similar to washing one's hands after returning from a burial. The bride's old self is buried with the marriage ceremony and she begins a new life "in the husband's house." This transition then becomes more significant for the woman than for the man, as the threshold ceremony is also a definition of territory by the husband's family. The new bride is "hedged in" by him and his people. The Akan's main interest in marrying off a daughter is in the daughter's duty and capacity to become a channel for ancestors to return through her offspring. At the marriage ritual, the Akan will feed eggs, a symbol of fertility, to the new bride.

BIRTHING

A marriage is not truly stabilized until all the prayers and the rituals have been completed and a woman gives birth. The birthing chamber and, in some cases, the house where a birthing is taking place are taboo to men. Men are strictly forbidden to share the secrets of childbirth. If the birthing is normal, no special rituals are required except for thanksgiving rites and "soul washing" to congratulate the soul of the woman for a job well done. The new mother is showered with gifts by her husband and relatives. However, if birthing is complicated, the woman in labor is encouraged to confess her sins; she may be accused of adultery and asked to name the illicit partner. Sacrifices may be made on her behalf to ensure a safe delivery. Needless to say, unnecessary fatalities have undoubtedly resulted from what is essentially a religious belief.

DEATH

The final ritual of passage, death, comes to women and men, alike and—apart from the absence of elaborate mourning by husbands—women's funerals are every bit as meticulously performed as men's. As departed spirits men and women are equally powerful, and an improper funeral for either might call down a great deal of trouble for the living. Because both male and female ancestors will be reincarnated, men and women alike must be honored in the prescribed manner so that they might return. Women's souls, however, do not demand the demeaning of their husbands in order that they may rest in peace. In the actual performance of funerary rites, men and women play prescribed and equally important roles based on their status in the family.

MOURNING

The death of a spouse marks another stage in the life of the individual, and separation rites are performed to terminate the coital rights of the deceased partner. Little has been recorded of rituals for the death of a wife, as these practices are minimal. Oral evidence indicates that a widower is encouraged to obtain a sexual partner as soon as possible in order to disgust the spirit of the deceased wife, who will then never again visit him.

In the case of a widow, however, it is assumed that a husband's soul will not rest until the widow has completed elaborate mourning rites and has been purified. Only then can she safely remarry. For most African women, mourning is an extremely intense period. The separation ritual to free the widow from her deceased husband is marked by purification rites that may involve acts like carrying hot coals to a stream for a pre-dawn ritual bath. For some women, it involves shaving a widow's hair, while others will require burning of all the clothes she wore at the time of her husband's death and those she wore during the period of mourning, which may last as long as a year. The widow can remarry only after completion of a formal mourning period followed by a "decent" length of time. Even at this stage the widow may not have a choice of husbands, as provisions may have been made for her to be inherited by her deceased husband's successor. If the widow refuses, she receives no material benefit from the marriage, except through her children if the society practices patrilineal inheritance.

Losing one's husband is viewed as extremely inauspicious, and this inauspiciousness is so contagious that among the Akan prior to purification none of the people who stream in to mourn with the bereaved family can shake hands with the widow. Widows bound by African religious traditions have undergone many unprintable customs. Widowhood, though, usually involves three main factors.

1. Surviving a husband attaches negative influences to the widow who may then contaminate others. This necessitates purification of the woman.

2. The spirit of the deceased husband stays with the widow until rites are performed to separate them. This separation is needed so that she can be safely passed on to another man. The unspoken assumption is that a woman must be married.

3. A man's soul can rest peacefully only when his spouse has meticulously observed all the rites of widowhood. Before his

spirit can rest in peace, a deceased man requires not only proper burial but also a thoroughly dejected widow who, at times, is thoroughly humilated by her in-laws.

At death, male sexuality shows a belligerent if not a malevolent character. These demeaning rites demanded of widows have been opposed by several groups over the years. Although the rites have been modified over time, the fundamental religious belief of inauspiciousness still remains, as do the socioeconomic and legal consequences of a system that gives widows no official status. In most African societies, female sexuality has no autonomous value outside of marriage and motherhood.

RITUALS: A MATTER OF RELIGIOUS BELIEF

At every stage in these passages through life, a principle of religion is involved. Since religion plays such a key role in enforcing societal norms and ethics, each stage has a social significance and reflects the status of women in the society and the relationships that exist between men and women. Participation in society is thoroughly imbued with these religous beliefs, even if they are not explicitly stated. Generally, African societies have more rituals for women than for men, perhaps reflecting their view of the greater spiritual strength of women. It seems, though, that many of these rituals are aimed at curbing the use of this strength, unless its use may benefit men. For example, several injunctions issued to men who are embarking on important tasks caution them to avoid women, thus reinforcing the belief that women shed negative influences. The failure of men to complete tasks is also attributed quite often to the unfaithfulness of a wife in their absence. Thus, men's incompetence may be blamed on ritual impurity occasioned by contact with women, women's lack of sexual fidelity, or even women's practice of witchcraft.

THE "BIO-LOGIC" OF RITUALS

Rituals for women, whether positive or negative, are related to procreation. The survival of the human race is dependent on its female component. The conclusion drawn in most African societies, however, is not that the female component should regulate the human community, but that everything should be done to ensure that the community is closely managed by the male component. Most African religious traditions have placed procreation at the center of the woman's universe; multitudes of taboos and rituals have evolved to direct her life and to keep her safe for procreation. Rituals of thanksgiving and congratulations are meticulously observed to ensure that a woman's soul is satisfied with her role in life. Birthing rituals of renewal and revitalization are performed after each parturition to prepare the female for the next pregnancy. Women's lives are regulated by their biology, as if their sole reason for being is to ensure that human life is reproduced and nurtured.

PARTICIPATION OF WOMEN IN RITUALS

As has been indirectly indicated above, most rituals are performed either on women or because of women. Among the Akan, for example, naming children is the prerogative of men because only men are deemed to have the capacity to be spiritual protectors. A second principle to be followed is that food and drink for the spirit world must be prepared by persons who are free from any flow of blood, which is sacred. Blood has a dual character; it is holy but it is also inauspicious when found where it should not be. As a result, women's participation in this ritual, as in others, is often limited.

In family rituals, men usually officiate, and menopausal women do so only *in extremis* or in supportive roles. Hence, among the Igbo of Nigeria, while a small boy can officiate at the ceremony of "splitting kola,"[3] a mature woman cannot. Recently when a woman was appointed a commissioner, men asked if they would now have to present drinks to her and have her split kola. This realization of the possibility of changing roles at least enables one to ask the question of "Why not?"

There are many very central cults from which women are excluded, except as clients. Women are forbidden to handle the instruments of divination. An important example is the exclusion of women in the Ifa divination, which, among the Yoruba, is the most important means of learning the will of the divinities. The will of the divinities is therefore communicated to individuals and to the community only through men. This seems to echo the reaction of the followers of Jesus of Nazareth when the women returned from the empty tomb with the message given to them by the risen Christ. The male response was, "These are idle tales told by women."

Parallel cults for men and women do exist, and both practice exclusion of the other sex. These generally pertain to areas of life that are gender-specific. But whereas the women's cults do not turn public to oppress men, the exclusively male cults do. For example, when newly circumcised boys parade through the villages and town of Tiriki in Kenya, or when Oro⁴ parades in the streets of Yoruba cities and towns, women must stay away. Huge processions of men snake through the streets of Ibadan during the Agemo Festival, terrorizing women. On occasion, these processions have been used specifically as camouflage to frighten women away from the market so their wares might be looted by men. Only recently have these processions been banned — at the insistence of women. It is worthwhile noting that the excesses of some exclusively male rituals are now being regulated by traditional rulers who see the incompatibility of these rituals with modern cosmopolitan communities.

Among the Akan, women feature prominently in ritual dances and singing, as in *mmommomme,* a war support ritual of singing that is specifically a female activity. When rituals are performed to show unity with the ancestors, women join in feasting and dressing up, but not in sacrificing. There is a prohibition, however, against women wearing masks, even when the ancestor being represented is a woman. Men have arrogated to themselves the prerogative of representing the spirits that shaped the history and destiny of the community. The exclusion of women from such community rituals has obvious political and social implications and may lie behind men's unwillingness to have women in positions of responsibility that include authority over men.

Purification rituals for women are more frequent. As mentioned above, women may undergo purification after a man's failure to accomplish a task, after a husband's death, or after childbirth. These purification rituals are very often prescribed by men diviners and performed on women by women. Women do take part in cathartic "mocking" rituals intended to release pent-up feelings against powerful personalities in the community. With little opportunity for real power, women throw themselves eagerly into these rituals to gain a sense of power or some "stolen" dignity.

Through its provisions for ritual, religion operates in the human community as a determiner of power, influence, domination, and oppression. This complex system of rituals makes a powerful statement to women about their self-worth and self-esteem. It is often an arena of intense passion, especially of fear, and hence an arena within which those in a weak position can with very little effort be made to give up their autonomy. If women more often than men find themselves in weaker roles in religion and ritual, they will require more attention if they are to be enabled and empowered toward full participation according to their innate abilities and acquired skills.

ISSUES FOR FURTHER RESEARCH

The religious emphasis on purity of sexual behavior to the exclusion of other moral and ethical "impurities," such as the motives that lead to excessive interest on loans or obscenely high profits on trade, is a sign of our special uneasiness about human sexuality. Until recently, this has been an area of silence. Christian thinkers who are concerned with a theology of creation should begin to break this silence and reexamine Christian fear of the "flesh."

Any discussion of impurity and righteousness, pollution and purification, or the link between the polluter and the polluted raises the question of the relationship between inauspiciousness and sexuality that links women with evil and makes men the innocent victims of women's sexuality. The issue of sexuality takes us back to the "Eve and evil" syndrome. The possibility has not been adequately examined that these stories of separation from God may simply mark a development in human consciousness toward further growth into autonomous beings who respond to God of their own free will. In the Akan tradition, the separation myth is not interpreted as sin that must be paid for by the "daughters of Eve." There is no call for purification through childbirth, nor for submission to the male.

The whole concept of auspiciousness and inauspiciousness is one that has been attached to sexuality by religious faiths. What constitutes inauspiciousness? Is it transmittable, and what has human sexuality to do with our "bad luck," if anything at all? In Africa, not only the African religious traditions but several Christian churches also operate with regulations that indicate a fear of pollution. Unfortunately the links between sexuality and "bad luck" are disabilities for women and obstacles put in the way of their development.

The African-instituted churches (AIC) that have done so much to involve women in their ministries still evoke the inauspiciousness of the energy that emanates from female sexuality and use it to curtail women's involvement. In the Aladura church, for example, four categories of people are not allowed into a house of prayer for fear that their presence might desecrate the holy place. They include a woman who has just delivered a baby, a menstruating women, men and women who have remained unwashed after sexual intercourse, and a woman with uncovered hair. The influences of African and Hebrew religions are obvious. While a man can be excluded on only one count, all four affect women. On the other hand, the same church gives special ritual significance to pregnancy. All pregnant women members must enroll in special prayer meetings within two months of their pregnancy. This ambivalence toward human sexuality crystalizes in the identification of woman-being with childbearing. Women, unfortunately, have accepted the idea that their "wholeness" depends exclusively on motherhood.

Women are often the keenest observers of these religious provisions against pollution, particularly in the case of menstruation. In African religion, loss of a life fluid is believed to defile a woman and all that she touches. The loss of blood is believed to render impotent or reduce the efficacy of any herbal medicine or talisman. Women understand that it is not in their interest to render either men or rituals impotent or, in the extreme, to cause the death of children, which ultimately may mean their own death. Women's knowledge brings with it responsibility. The association of public shame with impurity and of honor with the ability to cover up has fed the silence around human sexuality. These are matters of life and death, and all rituals are meticulously observed for the sake of the "wholeness" of the community.

HOLINESS AND THE WHOLENESS OF THE FEMALE

Much of the misinterpretation of African sexuality by Western anthropologists has its source in Western traditions of "prudishness." Prudish sexual norms have often been used by Western women to protect themselves from becoming a means of male gratification. To African women, on the other hand, sexuality has a religious function. Foremost in Asante regulations are those governing sexual relations, including several that oppose rape. Asante regulations include the following: a husband shall not force his wife to report adultery while they are in bed at night; a man shall not seduce a girl under the age of puberty; a woman shall not become pregnant before the initiation ceremony has been performed; a man shall not signal sexual interest to a married woman. There are also prohibitions against lewdness: no woman shall declare love to a man; no one shall refer to female sexual organs in the presence of the Queen Mother; no man shall seduce a woman in the bush nor any other place where there is no shelter; a man shall not seduce a woman near a hearth with the smoke of fire still coming out, near an earthenware pot holding water, or near a live chicken. Some of these taboos—such as the prohibition on a woman sitting in the male section of the royal house during her menses—are antipollution and intended to avoid the ritual contamination of that which is holy. In nearly all of these regulations, both male and female sexuality are held to be sacred and suspect at the same time.

On the other hand, there do not appear to be any myths, folktales, or proverbs that attribute inauspiciousness to menstruation. Neither do women seem to resent the limitation on their activities during their period. The restrictions may be inconvenient, but only marginally so compared with the impact of violations on the rest of one's life. The real issue here, however, is the exclusive focus of the personhood of a woman on her biological functions; this is generally not true of the male. Birth-giving, the first indication of "wholeness" of the woman, is also the event that calls her holiness into question. Giving birth indicates the wholeness of the woman in the same way that a woman's pregnancy stands for the wholeness of both the woman and the man. Although birthing ensures the continuity of the race, religion seems to have developed a tendency to assign "unholiness" to it, requiring purification of the woman after the birth has occurred. Forms of religion, including African religions and the various forms of Christianity in Africa that tend to perpetuate this way of thinking, should rethink these issues.

SEXUALITY, MARRIAGE, AND COVENANT

In Africa, where woman, marriage, and mother constitute an unbroken continuum, the question of sexuality cannot avoid the relationship of men and women in marriage. Where polygamy is accepted, there is an unspoken assumption that the female is to be a "monotheist" while the male acts as a "polytheist" arrogating to himself the freedom to worship the bodies of several women. "Proper" sexual relations for women are defined differently from the proper sexual activities of men. If we interpret sexual relations as the voluntary adoration of another's body, the distinction between "monotheist" and "polytheist" relations suggests a not completely fortuitous analogy between marriage and different forms of religion. Double standards toward sexual relations, resented by many women, seem to indicate that moving from "polytheism" to "monotheism" in marriage involves not only self-discipline but also evolution to a higher quality of relationship. If a woman's single-mindedness vis-à-vis her husband may mirror her total devotion to God in matters of religion, what is the significance of a man's tendency toward polygamy?

Polygamy is a very contentious issue in Africa, but has not, to my knowledge, been investigated from a religious point of view. Is there a correlation between "correct" sexual behavior as defined by the dominant society and that society's dominant thinking on "correct" religion? A study of polygamy, which Western Christians often view as a "hangover" from "primitive" lifestyles, may yield interesting information about its religious imperatives.

IN CONCLUSION

The concept of human sexuality cannot be examined apart from the total enterprise of struggling to understand our humanity. Sexuality is a central factor of being human and not a peripheral luxury for intellectual explication. It is so much a part of us that we fear it might compete with our sense of the presence of the Divine. In the past, this fear has prevented us from undertaking a serious celebration of sexuality. It has also engineered all sorts of ways of celebrating sexuality that burden females. A focus on sexuality in our time will help us break the silence on this subject that has had the effect in the past (and even today) of portraying human sexuality as a sinister factor and one that is antithetical to spirituality. An examination of African myths and rituals shows the integrated nature of the African concept of sexuality and spirituality. This is not a "women's issue." It is a community issue. It is also an issue that penetrates all religions.

As far as Africa is concerned, sexuality has been deemed a non-issue in the church, as in other Christian circles, except as the center of morality. We need to see sexuality as belonging to our experience and understanding of our humanity and of the church. An understanding of human sexuality can contribute as well to understanding the depth of the convenantal relations that the church seeks not only to symbolize but also to live. Men and women are sexually distinct beings who do not necessarily have to be identified with the opposite sex in marriage or in other forms of complementarity. Women are persons-in-com-munion, not persons who "complete" the other. There are female souls and there are male souls. We may need to reorient our thinking so that we see communion as a relationship devoid of hierarchical relations and power-seeking. When we have learned more about our humanity perhaps we will also be able to understand what God is telling us about divinity.

NOTES

1. Known in missiological circles as AIC (African Independent Churches), these churches have been founded and are led by Africans. Examples include the Aladura church in West Africa.

2. Africa has many different cultural traditions. It is interesting to note that among the patriarchal Yorubas, women do participate in giving names at these ceremonies.

3. The "kola" nut is often used in rituals among the Yoruba and Igbo. It indicates hospitality, sharing, and community.

4. Oro is the parading of the symbols of authority and communal discipline among the Yoruba. They are carried by night and are preceded by the sound of a bull's roar.

2

Christianity and African Women's Rituals

Rosemary N. Edet

INTRODUCTION

In all societies there are two types of mobility to which ritual is directed: role change and geographical movement. In both cases, the person undertaking the passage from one state to another must abandon certain attachments and habits and form new ones. They must, in other words, learn. Role changes occur more or less regularly and predictably in the life cycle of individuals, and although these role changes and their timing vary from one culture to another, they often maintain a general connection with physiological maturation. Birth, puberty, and death are universal objects of ritual, for at these times the individual enters into a new relationship with the world and the community, and they become subject to new opportunities, new dangers, and new responsibilities. In many African societies, however, other stages in the life cycle are ritualized: marriage, age-grades, professions, and so forth. And, of course, not all role changes can be easily fitted into a neat life-cycle framework.

Rosemary N. Edet, a Nigerian, is Senior Lecturer in the Department of Religious Studies and Philosophy at the University of Calabar, Nigeria. A religious sister, she holds a doctorate in Religion and Culture from the Catholic University of America, Washington, D.C.

The classic examples of rituals celebrated at the times of African women's role change are puberty, childbirth, marriage, and widowhood rituals. We will discuss two of these rituals, childbirth and widowhood, as they affect African women in their contemporary context. The discussion will center on these rituals as we reflect on them in the light of Christianity and human development in general.[1]

Women's rituals in Africa fall under ritual ideology which aims at controlling, in a conservative way, the behavior, the mood, the sentiment, and the values of women for the sake of the community as a whole. Much of the concern is to instruct, to direct, and to program individuals as they enter upon new tasks, and to stabilize society by preventing individuals from straying too far from the roles they have assumed. Much of the concern of ideology is with morality, ethics, and values; but these terms do not adequately cover the ritual phenomenon.

Ritual is a means by which humanity controls, constructs, orders, fashions, or creates a way to be fully human. Indeed, it gives meaning to the world, renews, and makes things right. It saves, heals, and makes whole again. Hence, ritual is necessary in our lives.

Elaborate ritual ceremonies for women include puberty, childbirth, and widowhood. Though some aspects of these rituals offend the sensibilities of Western observers and of some educated African women, traditionally the purpose of the ceremonies is to instill a more general set of values regarding the rights and duties of adulthood. Thus, in preparation for the dramatic culmination of women's rituals in Africa, there is generally a more protracted period of separation from the familiar household, which includes a variety of temporary and irksome taboos on food, bathing, and other creature comforts. The segregation always terminates in the outing ceremony in which the individual or group is exhibited for public view.

PUBERTY AND BIRTHING RITUAL

Some of the women's rituals embodied in religion and culture aid personal development, while others impede it. Since rituals are made up of symbols of primordial totality or dividedness, the symbols are sometimes polyvalent and have a strong influence on individuals and the community. In this essay, I will examine the rituals and religious experiences surrounding menstruation and birthing-blood impurity. I will show how women's experiences of potent rituals and symbols in Africa lead to theological reflections about symbol systems and provide vital religious resources.

Before discussing the rituals, it is only fitting that we discuss the taboo of blood impurity attached to them. This will help us to understand these rituals in their context.

The archetypal symbol of blood possesses an unusually tensive and paradoxical character. Its full semantic range comprises elements of both good and evil, the former being fairly clear but the latter relatively obscure and all the more ominous for its obscurity. It is understandable that on the positive side blood should connote life and hence power in various forms, including the strength and dignity of inheritance. But in most African societies, blood also has a more ominous significance which renders it taboo, that is, something to be dealt with ceremonially and on special occasions, not taken for granted and treated in a casual manner. Various explanations have been given for the taboo character of blood, especially blood issuing from the sexual organs of women. The most obvious is that since the spilling of too much blood produces death, blood becomes a symbol of death. Another explanation is that blood is associated with violence and with the sacred.[2] Thus blood is treated with awe and circumspection in all cultures, for it has a mysterious potency that can be dangerous unless properly handled.

Since blood is associated with the moments of death, birth, puberty, the physical aspect of marriage, and war, as well as with the more general idea of health and strength of life, it is very nearly coterminous with the rites of passage.[3] In connection with puberty and birth, women during menstruation and birth carry a contagion and require ceremonial cleansing. The same was true of warriors after battle.

Among most ethnic groups in Africa, menstrual blood is regarded as impure.[4] Menstruating women are segregated from the community and forbidden to touch objects of ceremonial usage, sometimes even their own food, for risk of contamination. They are forbidden to enter certain ceremonial shrines during the period. This stigma of impurity results from associating menstrual and birth blood with the danger of contact with spilled blood. Any act that sheds blood, except within a sacrificial act, is considered impure. This attribution of impurity to blood springs from the fact that wherever violence threatens, ritual impurity is present. Blood stains everything it touches with the color of violence and death. It is only natural, therefore, that women's blood should awaken fear, especially in men. However, although menstrual and childbirth bleeding can readily be distinguished from blood in murder or an accident, many societies regard it as the most impure of impurities. This extreme reaction has to do with the sexual aspect of both of these forms of bleeding. Sexuality is impure because it has to do with violence.[5]

To understand the impurity of menstrual and birthing blood we have to trace their relationship to blood spilled by violence as well as to sexuality. The fact that women's sexual organs periodically emit a flow of blood has always made a great impression on men, who have deep within their mythic consciousness a fear of women. Many ancient widely known mythical themes like vagina dentata, a snapping of the teeth, the conquering hero and the subdued maiden express the universal male fear of the castrating female. The myth passed into church history through the book of Tobit in the Scriptures (Tobit 3:7–8, 14–15, 8:1–9). In the story, the dangerous young woman is exorcized and the demon driven away. The crude earlier myth has been spiritualized, but in a direction dangerous for women. The myth with its accompanying themes or variations is also the subject of twentieth-century male dreams or fears. From this primal fear emerged the stories and figures that have been repeated from earliest times to the present all over the world.[6] They seem to confirm an affinity between sexuality and the diverse forms of violence that lead to bloodshed. Clitoridectomy practiced as part of puberty rites in some African societies is said to neutralize this fear.

Thus sexuality and violence have been associated over the course of several centuries. It is this association that lends an impure aspect to menstrual blood, which is seen as a physical representation of sexual violence. This process of symbolization is a response to some half-suppressed desire by men to place the blame for all forms of violence on women. By means of this taboo, this impurity, a transfer of violence has been affected and a monopoly established that is clearly detrimental to the female sex.

In traditional African religion and culture, as in other cultures and religions, the impurity of female blood has both religous and cultural roots. It is religious because it is blood spilled, even though outside the sacrificial act; cultural, because fear of women lies deep in the mythic consciousness of men. Blood impurity is handled both religiously and culturally in most African societies through rituals.

The puberty ritual celebrates and purifies menstrual blood impurity. During the ritual, clitoridectomy is sometimes performed with all its accompanying rites. The important elements here, as in birthing rituals, are segregation, purification, and exhibition. The outing day for a confined girl celebrates blood as dangerous and salvific; as contagious and efficacious; as a symbol of life and death. It is dangerous in that red explicitly symbolizes violence, killing, and, at its most general level of meaning, a breach in the social order. The symbolism suggests that the young woman is unconsciously rejecting her female role of motherhood, that in fact she is guilty. Indeed, this is why one African term for the menstrual period is etymologically connected with *ku-ba-ya* ("to be guilty").[7] Thus, in the Annang, Ibibio, and Ibo of Nigeria, the dominant color in the female puberty rite is red.[8] In this symbolism the procreative rather than the nutritive aspect of motherhood is stressed.[9] Today, in many urban areas in Africa, clitoridectomy is dying out, but the puberty rite still exists in a modified form. The persistence of this rite demonstrates the necessity of ritual in our lives.

BIRTHING RITUAL

At childbirth, a woman is segregated for a period of one month or more. The end of segregation is marked by the rites of purification and reintegration into the community, accompanied by feasting and exhibition.

Among certain ethnic groups in Nigeria, the purification rites take the following forms:

The senior sister-in-law waves a yam, cassava, or cocoyam tuber over the head of the mother and child and prays:

> *May everything that comes into this house be pleasant like this feast. No evil spirit shall assail the mother and her child, for I am now removing all evil spirits from this house.*

The yam, cassava, or cocoyam tuber or palm frond is thrown on the floor. In its place, a pot or a bottle of palm wine is taken and waved around the heads of all women present and these words recited:

> *May you conceive the next time you sleep with your husbands, so that we may all enjoy many similar feasts.*

Children from the neighborhood come with earthenware plates containing soup and yam; these are eaten outside the house and the plates broken into pieces. The symbolism of broken earthenware is to induce the ancestral spirits to reincarnate. After this, the children run to the stream and bathe themselves. Camwood is smeared on their bodies.

If the baby is a girl, a girl takes a mouthful of palm wine and spits it on the fire in the new mother's hearth. If the baby is a boy, a boy performs this ritual act. The act is repeated until the fire goes out. The new mother then sweeps out the whole house, including the ashes from the hearth, while the girls fetch fresh fire from the neighboring house. This is a purification rite using the death/life motif in the fire rite and the cleansing of ritual impurity in the sweeping rite, in which the old/new motif recurs.

After the rite, the girl puts some chalk on the baby's head and says:

> *If your parents send you a message, do not refuse, but if a spirit sends you one, say that you have no feet. Let nothing that your parents eat cause any harm to you.*

The above is the rite of incorporation of the baby into the family and community.

The following day, the girl returns and escorts the mother to the farm, where the latter touches a yam tendril, cassava leaves, or cocoyam leaves and says:

Today the taboo against my touching yams, cassava, and cocoyam has been removed.

The above mentioned rites take place after twenty-eight days of seclusion, and are followed by the public exhibition of mother and child, accompanied by some feasting.[10]

WIDOWHOOD RITUAL

Bereavement offers a similar basis for ritual action. When an individual to whom the living were emotionally attached in a positive or negative way, or both, has died, an emotional separation must be achieved. The departed and the survivors must be released from each other; otherwise the living will remain miserable in their frustrated devotion, and the departed soul will be unhappy. Once again, the goal of rituals is to separate effectively the living from the dead, to accomplish the transition, to bring about the incorporation of the dead into his or her proper place in the hereafter, and to reunite the mourners with each other and with the community. That this passage be satisfactorily completed is always a matter of community interest. Widowhood rituals are aimed at terminating the socially destructive and self-destructive period of mourning by bereaved survivors.[11]

Among most African communities, the death of a husband heralds a period of imprisonment and hostility to the wife or wives. This treatment may or may not be out of malice, but in all cases, women suffer and are subjected to rituals that are health hazards and heart-rending.

Among the Efiks of the Cross River State in Nigeria, at the death of a husband, the wife is accused of killing her husband. The accusation is usually made by sisters-in-law whose cordial attitude changes at the news of their brother's death. The wife's hair is loosened and made very untidy; she is dressed in a very old dress and a wrapper. Bathing is taboo. Verbal attacks keep her weeping all the time, and she is expected to cry for her husband three times a day, publicly and audibly, at dawn, noon, and evening. The children are taken away by their aunts, who may not take care of them; neither is the mother allowed to take care of them. The widow is also forbidden to eat, and she is never to leave the family house until the period of mourning is over, after which she wears a black dress for months. After the stipulated period of mourning, there is an end-of-mourning ceremony. It is only after this "outing" that she functions normally outside her home. Since she has no right of inheritance, she can either go back to her family or establish herself on her own if she is an industrious woman. She now assumes the total parental responsibilities for her children, becoming to them both father and mother.

RITUALS: POSITIVE OR NEGATIVE?

Since our interest is in women affected by these rituals, the questions that come to mind are: Do these rituals oppress women or promote their welfare? What are their positive and negative points? Do the positive aspects fit within the Christian perspective? What has Christianity been able and unable to do about these rituals?

It is obvious from the description of the rituals that they have both positive and negative aspects and so promote as well as hinder women's growth and development. The oppressive aspects of the childbirth ritual described above are: it imparts ritual impurity and guilt to the act of bringing forth new life; it deprives the women of nutritious meals which they need after giving birth, and thus creates health hazards; the segregation deprives women of rights of movement and of the ability to seek medical or other needed help; and the rites create a sense of inferiority and self-depreciation—they subjugate women and deprive them of self-worth.

On the positive side, childbirth rituals are occasions of

thanksgiving, joy, and celebration, as the prayers during the rites indicate. This aspect of the ritual gives the mother a sense of accomplishment and inclusiveness. The mystery of giving birth is the woman's discovery that she is on that plane of life which amounts to a religious experience untranslatable in terms of masculine experience. It is not the natural phenomenon of giving birth that constitutes the mystery, but the revelation of the feminine sacredness that is the mystic unity between life, woman, nature, and the divinity. This revelation is of a transpersonal order and is therefore expressed in symbols and actualized in rites. The young mother becomes conscious of a sanctity that emerges from the innermost depth of her being, and this consciousness, obscure though it may be, is experienced in symbols. It is in realizing and living this sacredness that a woman finds the spiritual meaning of her own existence; she feels that life is both real and sanctified. Thus, at the base of every female rite is a profound religious experience, which gives access to the sacred.[12]

The essential rite, then, is the solemn exhibition of mother and child to the family and the community. This is a ceremonial announcement that the mystery has been accomplished. To show something ceremonially, whether a sign, an object, or a person, is to declare a sacred presence, to acclaim the miracle of a hierophany. The collective dance and feasting express the same experience in a way that is at once more flexible and more dramatic.

The positive aspects of childbirth rituals in Africa fit within the Christian custom of thanksgiving to the Creator for the good things of life, and especially life itself. Mary took her child to the temple, and so have numerous Christian mothers throughout the ages. The act acknowledges God as the author of life and woman as cocreator. Thus the exhibition of mother and child actually acknowledges the presence of God with God's people. This aspect of the ritual should be capitalized upon by Christianity through admission of the fact that women are God-bearers, and as such can be ministers of the word and sacraments. They are not inferior to men, neither are they impure when performing their natural God-given duty of birthing. The church is called mother. Is she performing her function of birthing in Africa?

The Bible talks of the "pangs of birth" as a symbol of the eschatological pains. The pain in both cases is temporal, for it gives place to the joy of new life. One has to die to the old in order to live anew. Thus death and life are two aspects of life. Every rite expresses the coexistence of the contraries or *coincidentia oppositorum.*

The taboo of blood impurity lies at the root of the ecclesiastical symbols of women in most of our religious denominations (except for a few of the New Religious Movements founded by women) that operate solely on paternal symbols; hence they are one-sided and ineffective in an age when paternalism is challenged. Maternal symbols, when recognized, appreciated, and shared as important assets in community and personality development, can restore a balance to humanity. Therefore it is vital in today's church and society that feminine religious experiences be taken into serious consideration in both church- and nation-building.

Maternal symbols are that of primordial totality, of universal harmony, of the vital source of happiness. This is confirmed by the findings of Carl Jung. According to Jung, the maternal element is the original basis and profound source of all psychic life. The child aspires to return to the maternal womb in order to be reborn again to new life. Hence womanhood enters into the concept of God. Indeed, religion is guided by the desire to be born to oneself and rediscover one's own total integrity.[13]

WHERE DOES THE CHURCH STAND?

A cursory look at the widowhood ritual reveals only one positive aspect: the transition or separation of the living from the dead. Apart from this, the ritual reinforces despair; it breaks up the family into warring factions, renders the widow helpless, creates health hazards, disturbs the children's psychological growth, and leaves the family insecure. In fact, it portrays death as the end of life. Hence the widowhood ritual is totally opposed to Christian principles of life and love. The hostility in this case constitutes a grave offense because it comes from women who may become widows themselves. This ritual creates a division among women to their own detriment and as such is a disintegrating factor in the community.

As far as I know, Christianity has not directly addressed the effects of this ritual on women until recently, when Christian women in Imo State, Nigeria, organized a seminar on widowhood ritual in an effort to improve the life of women in rural areas. This came under the auspices of the government's Nigerian "Better Life for Rural Women" program. For the first time, men came to realize the burden that women carry as part and parcel of their cultural heritage. Three years ago, the Catholic Women organization in Calabar Diocese organized a seminar in which the same issue was discussed in the context of women's ritual and Christian liturgy. This is a consolation to concerned African churchwomen, because African women are beginning to be aware of themselves as human beings and as partners to men and want to be treated as such.

The Christian proclamation of human liberation and the equality of men and women is indeed good news for women, but this teaching is more theoretical than practical. If it were practical, Christianity could have emancipated women from adverse rituals. I am not denying the fact that African women have benefitted from the Good News. What I am saying is that Christianity legalizes and reinforces the oppression of women and their subjugation to men in all aspects of life. The old adage that "women should be seen and not heard" is taken over by the churches and given a biblical foundation in the first letter to the Corinthians. This also affects ecclesial structures so that women are excluded from the ordained ministry and administrative roles of the church and thus remain outsiders in the church.

The church as the Body of Christ, People of God, and primordial sacrament has its rituals or sacraments that operate alongside traditional rituals of childbirth and widowhood. The values that prompt and sanction the performance of ritual are also, generally speaking, the same values that motivate people in their daily lives. But because the values that are recognized by religion may also include the sacred goal of spiritual salvation, the church should explore traditional rituals and infiltrate them with its values.

Through its rituals the church in its members shares at all

times in the salvation promised by God. This promise of salvation comes through Christ as God's Word, and it is wrought by
God through Christ as the mediator. In the rite of the churching
of women and in its funeral rites, the church should give concrete form to its own nature, which is to be the eschatological,
historical, and social presence of God's self-communication to
the world. This it does for the sake of the salvation of its members. Since the rites exist through the Word and in the Word,
they are themselves Word. It is the Word that provides the rites
with their terms of reference, making the action relevant to the
special circumstances of our lives, hence the prominent place
accorded to the Word of God in the church's rites. The Word
is the dominant symbol in all the church's rites, a permanent
saving power.[14]

The fact that the church has rites underscores the necessity
of rituals in our lives. Rituals are the sacramental self-realization
of the individual or the church and are thus indispensable. All
the church's rites of passage and its healing rites are rooted in
Scripture. This makes it mandatory for the church or Christianity to address itself to African women's rituals so that the
saving and liberating power of the Word may liberate women
from unnecessary psychological, economical, and political shack-
les. Jesus the Christ, the Word of God, reconciles us to the
Father. Our brokenness is healed by repentance and forgiveness.
The church's concern about the welfare of women can stop
harmful traditional rituals and replace them with the church's
rites instead of allowing them to operate on parallel levels.

Regarding the childbirth ritual which operates alongside the
churching of women, the church should incorporate into its rites
positive aspects of the traditional ritual so that the whole community is involved when a new member arrives. The churching
of mothers should be rid of its purificatory aspect. That is, the
church should not regard mothers at childbirth as unclean and
thus to be purified. The whole rite should be that of thanksgiving
and celebration, during which our alienation from God, society,
and self is acknowledged and even proclaimed. Thus the bipolar
tension of life is met by the simultaneous acceptance of wholeness and infirmity, deprivation and restoration, alienation and
reconciliation. The feeling of a share in divine activity should

proceed from an encounter with the Word within the church as a healing community and with its members as the bearers of healing power. The minister within this context is a healer as bearer of the Word. The Word is also in the mother and in all women members of the church as priestly, kingly, and prophetic people; therefore there should be women ministers, women who have actually experienced a share in the divine activity of creation. This is the only way of liberating women and promoting their growth and development as mature members of the church that heals.

Jesus was a revolutionary. He liberated the woman with the issue of blood and restored the son of the widow of Nain. He never tortured them, nor segregated them, nor demanded purification rites. As long as we continue to perform these rituals in their traditional forms, the Word has no chance of being good news to African women in certain aspects of their lives. The church should be interested in women's rituals as a means of understanding the mentality of African women, because rituals show us that the true person, the spiritual person, is not given, is not the result of a natural process; rather, she is "made," in accordance with models revealed by divine beings and preserved in myths and rituals. The priestesses are spiritual elites of our societies. It is they who know the world of the spirit, the truly human world. Their function is to reveal the deep meaning of existence to individuals, and to help them assume the responsibility of being truly human and thus of participating in religion and culture. It is this inclusiveness that generates the sense of belonging as an active mature adult with rights and privileges. The church has not extended this type of inclusiveness to women—hence our brokenness, which is the brokenness of humanity.

Furthermore, after hundreds of years of British, German, French, and Italian colonization of Africa, despite our predominantly female population we have only a handful of women ministers of the Word and sacraments. The churches continue to choose their leaders from the educated, predominantly male, middle classes. There are no women bishops. In local churches, women are teachers who do not participate to any great extent in the church's theological and political discussions, and whose views are not taken into account. Our churches reject prostitutes, single mothers, and, in many churches, women revolutionaries and intellectuals.[15]

As a concerned African woman, I wish to remind the churches that women are part of the People of God and the Body of Christ. We are called to freedom and salvation. The People of God are at the same time the mystery of the presence of the risen Christ and the sociological expression of human activity at a particular time in history. We are part of that people and, as such, we are on the move, both in the historical process and transcendentally, toward a *kairos* which has been proclaimed. As women, we feel our scope for movement is restricted and reduced by human sinfulness, which has created structures in which some people have domination over others. Our responsibility is to go forward with the people, to reaffirm from revelation our own liberation as *imago Dei* called to an equal status with men and united in the community of all who believe in Christ, and as sensitive and thinking women who have received the message of salvation and can effectively proclaim that message to all humanity. This responsibility includes going forward with the People of God in its struggle for liberation and for salvation which must be expressed in signs of life, love, and solidarity.[16]

NOTES

1. Anthony F. C. Wallace, *Religion: An Anthropological View* (New York: Random House, 1966), 127.

2. Philip Wheelwright, *Metaphor and Reality* (Bloomington and London: Indiana University Press, Indiana, 1978), 113–14; cf. René Girard, *Violence and the Sacred* (Baltimore and London: John Hopkins University Press, 1981), 33.

3. Arnold van Gennep, *The Rites of Passage* (Chicago: University of Chicago Press, 1960).

4. The Ibibios and the Quas of the Cross River State observe the taboo. Rural women still stay home from church or any social function of religious significance during their menstrual period. Christian women stay home from church for a month or more after childbirth. At the church, a ritual called "Churching of Mothers" is performed at the entrance of the church before they enter the building.

5. Girard, *Violence and the Sacred,* 34.

6. Verrier Elwin, "The Vagina Dentata Legend," *British Journal of Medical Psychology* 19 (1943): 439–53; cf. Wendy D. O'Flaherty, *Asceticism and Eroticism in the Mythology of Siya* (London: Oxford University Press, 1973), 187; and Marcel Griaule, *Conversation with Ogotemueli: An Introduction to Dogon Religious Ideas* (London: Oxford University Press, 1965), 158.

7. *Kubaya* is Ndembu language derived from the word *mbayi* meaning menstruation.

8. The color red is used by the Ibibio and Annang in the form of red camwood, dye, or palm oil with which the bodies of the girls are painted.

9. Mircea Eliade, *Myths, Dreams and Mysteries* (Great Britain: Harvill Press, 1960), 230.

10. Emefie Ikenga-Metuh, *Comparative Studies of African Traditional Religions* (Onitsha: Imico Publishers, 1987), 114–17.

11. Wallace, *Religion: An Anthropological View,* 130.

12. Eliade, *Myths, Dreams and Mysteries,* 215.

13. Carl Jung, *The Portable Jung,* ed. Joseph Campbell (New York: The Viking Press, 1976), 167.

14. Rosemary N. Edet, *Revision of the Church's Rites* (unpublished paper, Washington, D.C., 1982).

15. Aracely De Rochietti, "Women and the People of God," in *Through Her Eyes,* ed. Elsa Tamez (Maryknoll, New York: Orbis Books, 1989), 116–17.

16. Ibid., p. 117.

3

Christianity and the African Rituals of Birth and Naming

Anne Nasimiyu-Wasike

INTRODUCTION

In all African ethnic groups one finds rituals that mark the peak moments in people's lives—for example, rituals that mark one's birth, naming, initiation into adulthood, marriage, and death. These peak moments in one's life are sometimes referred to as an individual's "life crises" or "rites of passage" (Van Gennep, 7). They all have three main phases: separation (preliminal), transition (liminal), and incorporation (postliminal). These rites change one's status or social position in society. They are present in various ways in all human societies, since there are distinctions of status in every society and each human individual is moving from one position to another during the course of his or her life.

The Christian rites—for example, baptism, marriage, and funerals—have the major characteristics of the "rites of pas-

Anne Nasimiyu-Wasike, a religious sister from Kenya, is Senior Lecturer in the Department of Philosophy and Religious Studies at Kenyatta University, Nairobi. She has a doctorate from Duquesne University, Pittsburgh, Pennsylvania.

sage." In this study I would like to establish a dialogue between Christian infant baptism and the African rite of birth and naming. In some communities, some of these African rituals have been overshadowed or taken over by Western Christian rites, while other communities have insisted on carrying out two rites—the African rite and the Western Christian rite. Since the Second Vatican Council a new awareness was initiated in the church. The Council Fathers acknowledged that culture is of central importance in the communication of the gospel message. Christianity has the duty to take all peoples and their cultures seriously. It must endeavor to meet the challenge of knowing people in all their diversity and mutability. Christ the incarnate Word of God is the restorer of all cultures from brokenness and disintegration to wholeness and integration.

Thus Christianity is charged with the responsibility and duty of evangelizing cultures through a gradual process which denounces evil structures within those cultures and gives a Christian interpretation to the customs, morality, and religious character of those cultures. God is our primordial example in the process of inculturation or evangelization of cultures. First of all, we know that God chose to communicate God's self to us in Jesus Christ through a particular culture (Nasimiyu). Jesus Christ was a true Galilean from Nazareth, and from there he went about his ministry, denouncing whatever enslaved the people and rejecting anything that kept the people from appreciating their fundamental human dignity. Christ's message was a challenge to some of the cultural structures and systems, especially those which legitimized the exploitation of others in order to preserve the privileged status, power, and prestige of a few.

Another reality that we are aware of is that the gospel message has been communicated to us through a particular cultural context. The thought forms, syntax, and symbols of that culture were employed in formulating the gospels. These two factors give us a model that we have to follow in searching for new ways of interpreting the gospels and translating them into all cultures, so that they become truly rooted in any given culture.

This study will limit itself to the investigation of the African rituals of birth and naming and how these relate to Christianity, or how they can be integrated into the Christian rituals of infant baptism.

THE AFRICAN RITE OF BIRTH

In various African communities the birth of the first child has a threefold significance. First of all, it introduces a new member to the community. Secondly, the young mother attains her honorific title of Madam *Omukelema* in Lubukusu of Kenya, thereby joining the ranks of all respectable women of the clan and becoming worthy of consideration as an adult by the community. Women who cannot have children for one reason or another are not accorded that respect and honor. Thirdly, through the birth of the first child, both parents of the new baby acquire the status of parenthood. Traditionally, the more children the parents have, the greater their privileges and prestige in the community.

The ritual of birth commences with the pregnancy of the mother and reaches its climax at birth. Traditionally, when a woman becomes pregnant, she tells her husband who respects and honors her. The husband announces the good news only to the relatives. The whole pregnancy is referred to in a symbolic manner. For example, among the Babukusu, the pregnant woman is referred to as the one "with blood" (*ali ne kamafuki*). The term "child" is not used, in order to protect the expectant mother from any psychological, physical, and ritual harm, and also to deceive the bad spirits who may be jealous and envious of the Supreme Being's blessing upon the couple. In this reality, the Supreme Being's omnipotence becomes symbolically tangible. The pregnant woman is instructed in the rituals and rules that she has to observe in order to ensure easy and safe delivery and to protect herself and the child.

In some communities, there are ceremonies to pray for and to bless the expectant mother. For example, among the Babukusu, a ritual of "well-wishing" (*Khung'asia*) is performed, especially for expectant mothers who are having problems with their pregnancy (Wagner, 299). The husband or the father of the wife provides a hen for the ceremony. These two persons are chosen because it is through them that the young wife is joined to the clan of her husband and to the clan of her father. The woman's legal protection passes from her father to her husband at marriage.

The ritual is performed by the pregnant woman's father-in-law. He invites his daughter-in-law to stand in the homestead in the presence of all the relatives who have gathered for this celebration. The father-in-law waves the live hen over the pregnant woman's whole body, while imploring the Creator, *Wele Khakaba,* the molder of all human life, to bless and give good health to the pregnant woman and the child in her womb. This ritual is supposed to bring God's protection, good fortune, and good health upon the pregnant woman and the expected child (Wagner, 299).

The father-in-law assumes the priestly role in this ritual. Usually the senior elder in the homestead performs the priestly functions. This ritual of "well-wishing" to the pregnant mothers could be christianized and made into a sacrament. This is not a new sacrament, but rather the reestablishment of a ritual that was in the Church before Vatican Council II (*Collectio Rituum,* 391–395).

The "well-wishing" ceremony could be held twice a year for all healthy expectant mothers, but for those who are having problems and are sickly, the ritual could be held at any time and as often as desired. The ritual could be performed by the elder of the homestead if he is a Christian, or by a village catechist or a priest. Instead of a hen, holy water in a calabash could be sprinkled onto the expectant mothers, using feathers or a cow tail. Just as it is believed that any evil that may be disturbing the pregnant mother leaves and enters the hen, so do Christians believe that holy water drives away evil powers and strengthens and protects the one who uses it. The African prayers could be used together with other prayers: for example, the old Christian "Blessing of a Woman before the Birth of a Child" (*Collectio Rituum,* 391, see the appendix).

The child's birth is hailed with great joy throughout the whole village. The community participates in the rituals, because through the birth of a child, the whole community is blessed by God.

The midwife is the first person who prays over the child, wishing her or him peace and happiness in this world. After the child is washed and wrapped in a baby shawl, the midwife hands the baby to its mother with a prayer. For example, in Zaire she prays, "The midwife cannot eat the child, what she eats is meat and salt." (Lwakale, 29). And the baby's mother responds: "Give her/him to me truly." Here the mother affirms the words spoken by the midwife by saying, "Let it be done to my Nafula (or any other pet name the mother has chosen for the child) as you so wish."

During their formation, Christian midwives could be taught to respect and revere human life as the most sacred of all God's creation. The midwife could be taught prayers to welcome the child at the child's birth, so that the birthing becomes a sacramental experience.

The birth of a new baby is rightly called a "Rite of Passage." Parrinder defines "Rites of Passage" as "those traditional rituals which mark stages in the life of an individual, passing from one stage to another though a sacred event" (Parrinder, 79). At birth, mother and child discontinue their previous association. They die to the old state of pregnancy of being as one, are now alive in another state of existence, and are risen in the new life of journeying toward total incorporation into the community (Mbiti, 113).

During the confinement period, life is suspended in the village, as Mbiti recounts:

> The forbidden washings, cleaning of houses and moving of fire from one house to another symbolize the halting of normal life, the death of corporate life in expectation of new rhythm of life represented in the birth of the child. In the birth of a child, the whole community is born anew; it is revived and revitalized. (Mbiti, 115)

The end of confinement is marked by great ceremonial feasting and rejoicing. The mother and child go through the rituals of purification and incorporation into the community. The mother and child take fresh baths and have their hair shaved off to symbolize and dramatize the death of one state and rising again to another. As Mbiti notes:

> The hair represents her pregnancy, but now that this is over old hair must be shaved off to give way to new hair, the symbol of new life. She is now a new person. . . . The hair also has the symbolic connection between the mother and child, so that shaving it indicates that the child now belongs not only to her but the entire body of relatives, neighbours, and other members of the society. She has no more claim over the child as exclusively her own: the child is now "scattered" like shaved hair so that it has a hundred mothers, a hundred fathers, a hundred brothers and hundreds of other relatives. (Mbiti, 115)

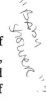

Relatives and friends bring gifts for the mother and father of the baby as a sign of community participation in the formation, protection, cultivation, and creation of the new life that God the Great Provider has given to the society. This celebration of welcoming new life in the community is still being cherished by many ethnic communities. This value could be recaptured and maximized by the Christian faith.

The traditional ritual of the mother and child's coming out of seclusion has three main steps. First of all, the mother presents the child to the sun for the first time. Standing in the doorway, the young mother invites the child to greet the sun which is the symbol of divinity, the source of life and fecundity.

Secondly, the child is placed on the ground so that he or she is in touch with the soil. The soil is a symbol of nourishment for the child, and it also symbolizes that the child is now public property, totally free from the mother. The child now belongs to the whole community. The child's kinship bonds are now established and his or her ties to one person or one household are symbolically destroyed (Mbiti, 113). Now the whole community is responsible for feeding the child and providing him or her with all the necessary things for a balanced growth.

Thirdly, the mother sprinkles the child with some water. This is a symbol of rain which is necessary for the seed to germinate and grow. The mother prays to the Creator-Provider of all life

to protect and safeguard the new child. She implores the Creator, the Author of life, the great Ancestor, to grant good health and strength so that the baby may grow well under the Creator's protection. Addressing the baby she prays, "May you grow like finger-millet which ripens quickly and in a short time and not like maize which grows very slowly and takes a long time to ripen" (Wagner, 308). This ritual expresses the plenitude of life and consecrates the new life to the Creator, the Provider and Source of all life.

The final step is that of anointing with ghee (oil). The mother, father, and their new baby sit together in the doorway of their house facing the assembled visitors. A young virgin girl especially chosen anoints the mother on the forehead and the palm of the right hand and then does the same to the baby. The father anoints his face and passes the oil to his mother. The mother anoints her feet and passes the remainder of the oil to the young girl who anoints herself.

Anointing symbolizes the seal of the covenant by which the young mother is fully incorporated into the ethnic community of her husband as an adult and is also consecrated to the Creator, the Great Provider. The child's anointing is a sign of consecration to the Creator and the community's solid acknowledgment that the new person is one with them in all things. The anointed members are the immediate protectors of the new life. The new child is a bond which now ties the two families together, the family of the child's mother and the family of the child's father. This ritual could be incorporated into infant baptism. Jesus Christ becomes the new light, who is the source of life and regeneration. The local Christian community becomes the symbol of nourishment for the child. The child will draw his or her moral, spiritual, mental, and physical education and nurturing from this local Christian community. Therefore, the local Christian community must be made fully aware of this responsibility.

The third symbol used in the African ritual is water. For the Africans, water is a symbol of life, whereas to the Christians, water is a symbol of both death and life. By immersion into water at baptism, the individual dies to the old life of sin and rises to the new life of the children of God. Here the new life in Jesus

Christ could be emphasized over and above the new physical life of the new child. The Christian anointing of the new child could be used instead of the African anointing.

Usually the ceremony ends with a big communal meal. This too could be incorporated into the rite of infant baptism. At the communal meal, the relatives present their gifts to the parents of the new child. The gift-giving is a sign that the young mother and father are valued by their parents and relatives, that their relatives are generous and caring towards the new family link that has been established through the new child, and that they will always support them. The fact emphasized could be that as Christians a new family in Jesus Christ is formed and this is now the new extended family which should care and support any new member of it.

THE RITE OF NAMING

There are various rites of naming in different African communities. For example, among the Babukusu of Kenya, one is given three different types of names in his or her lifetime. The first is the "ancestral name." The second is the childhood name, given by the mother when she holds the baby in her arms for the first time. In addition, each Mubukusu has the adolescent name.

Only the ancestral name is ceremonially bestowed upon the child. This name is carefully chosen, and its bestowal is connected with particular circumstances. A boy is named after his circumcision but before the last rite of his initiation into adulthood, and a girl is named at the betrothal feast. The majority of the people are named in their infancy.

The ancestral name is chosen by the child's father or the maternal uncle in consultation with a diviner if necessary. A child may be named after anybody whom the family believes needs to be remembered in a living manner. If a paternal or maternal grandparent dies while the mother is pregnant, the child will automatically be named after him or her. The female children are strictly named after female persons and the male children after male persons.

A child may also be named after two persons, if necessary.

One is addressed as the "head" and the other as the "servant." In order to determine who is the "head" and who is the "servant," two chickens, a brown one and a white one, are thrown on the roof of the house by the child's father. The one that comes down first is the "servant" and the one that stays on the roof or comes down last is the "head." The task of protecting the child is thus divided between the two spirits. The mother sits in the doorway facing the rear of the house, with the baby in her lap covered with a blanket. The uncle stands in front of the child, sips some beer from a new gourd, and spits it against the blanket, calling the name of the ancestral spirit and imploring him or her to come and protect the child and not feel lonely and neglected. If the child is to be named after two spirits, the maternal uncle and the paternal uncle perform the ritual together, calling upon the spirits of both to promote the child's good health.

After the prayer, the uncle slips a wristlet made of iron or skin over the right hand of a baby boy or over the left hand of a baby girl. A wristlet is a symbol of the child's consecration to the Creator and to the ancestor spirits (Wagner, 313). The new name links the child to the ancestor and indicates the origin of one's personality.

The celebrant prays for peace and richness to come and dwell in the household and admonishes the evil spirits and people of evil looks not to come near the new child. For the child is born neither of earthly being, nor of a ghost, nor of sorcery, but of the Creator, the Great Provider. For the child the celebrant prays:

> May this child live only according to the precepts of the Creator, who makes the sun rise and set, who calls people and gives them strength to beget children. It is only for you, you alone Master-Creator Spirit that we clap hands. (Lwakale, 19)

Christian infant baptism could add a special prayer to the ancestor spirit or patron saint whose name is chosen for the new baby. The stress should be laid on the protection of the child from the evil spirits, sorcery, and witchcraft by the Creator through the ancestor spirits.

Some Africans acquire new names at different stages in life or when they acquire new status in society. As Celestin Mubenganyi Lwakale has noted:

> It is even normal that for each new period of life, a new name is adopted which is one with the person. These are names which must always remain because they are "names from the internal." There are others which are renounced because they are linked to different situations of our existence. Those who have performed the initiation ceremonies have *ipso facto* modified their personalities; it is then normal that they bear a new link to their initiation which is destined to remind them of the day they accepted to play a new role in the community. (Lwakale, 67)

The ancestral names are "names from the internal" that not only continue the physical line of life, but have a religious focus of keeping the departed relatives in the state of personal immortality (Mbiti, 121).

Since it is prohibited to pronounce the ancestral name among some communities except in serious circumstances, a child must be named with other names. For example, among the Babukusu new names are imposed at various stages, for instance, to symbolize the reinforcement and the newness of the life that one has embraced. This idea is similar to Christian belief, and it could be integrated so that we have one African Christian infant baptism instead of African rites of birth and naming and Christian infant baptism. The ceremony of the ancestral name could be incorporated into the Christian infant baptism, thus giving the child two names, one of which corresponds to the childhood name or the first name bestowed on the child by his or her mother. The mother gives whatever pet name she wishes to the child. The pet names have no mystical meaning, but they tell one something about the bearers of the names. For example, if the birth occurs during a rainy day, a girl child is named Nafula or a boy Wafula. (Most names among the Babukusu often take the prefixes "Wa" for the boys' names and "Na" for the girls' names.) The names Nafula and Wafula mean "rainy" or "rain." The child may also be named after a significant social, religious, or political event happening at the time of his or her birth. In addition, individuals continue to acquire new names if they perform a remarkable and outstanding feat. The name indicates a personality change that one has undergone.

CONCLUSION

The African (Babukusu) rites of birth and naming have several similarities with Christian infant baptism. First of all, the African rites mark the passage of the child into this world and the young mother from girlhood to motherhood, whereas Christian baptism celebrates passage into the new life of Christ. Secondly, the African rites incorporate the individual into the clan and the community of adults, and the Christian rite welcomes the initiate (child) into the church, the People of God, the community of believers.

Thirdly, the African rites are fundamentally a community affair, since they take place in the community and are of the community. Infant baptism stresses the communal aspects of the Christian rite and should thus concern the entire local parish community.

Fourthly, the African naming of the ancestral name is marked with celebrations, and the names have special significance in relation to their bearers, while the Christian naming signifies the new life that the individuals have embarked upon.

Finally, the symbol of life and death prevails as the most outstanding metaphor in the African rites (Floro, 42). Similarly, the celebration of the death and resurrection of Christ Jesus is central to baptism and to Christian faith.

The similarities that exist between African and Christian rituals could be integrated in order for the Christian message to build on African values and institutions, so that it brings them to perfection and completion and elevates them to universal status in the Church.

In the process of integrating Christian with African rituals, both rituals will benefit (Nasimiyu, 66–72). The Christian ritual will be enriched by African values, and the African ritual will acquire a universal meaning by the church's incorporation of its creative symbolism into its liturgy and catechesis. This will be one way in which the African people will continue to express the crucial experiences of their life cycle in the modern world in which social changes are displacing the traditional rituals.

In transforming the African way of life, the message of Christ will gradually give birth to a truly African church. Commenting on this process, F. Eboussi Boulaga says:

[The message of Christ comes into a culture to] fulfill the dream of a life in all its fullness, a life destined to triumph even in the collapse of the framework of a way of life that had been consecrated from time immemorial.

Hence the coming of Christ bears on the lot of the group as such, and it transposes itself into, passes into a Church. The continuity is there — the continuity of a life undergoing a meta-morphosis in depth. (Eboussi Boulaga, 64)

APPENDIX

The Rite of Well-Wishing
(Blessing of Expectant Mothers)

Leader:	Our help is in God the Great Provider
All:	Who made heaven, earth, and all things.
Leader:	Come and protect your servant
All:	Who trusts in you, O God the Great One.
Leader:	Be a source of strength for her, O God,
All:	Against the attacks of the evil spirits.
Leader:	Let the evil spirits have no power against her,
All:	And let all the evil eyes turn away from her.
Leader:	Send her your power and grace to help her,
All:	And may your Eye watch over her.
Leader:	O God, the Great Provider, hear our prayer,
All:	And let my cry come to you.

Leader: May the spirit of God be with you.
All: Amen.

Let us pray. O God our strength, our power, and our comfort, you called your servant, N., to acknowledge you in faith. May her constant commitment to you ever strengthen her against all evil power, witches, and sorceries.

O God, Creator of all things, mighty and awe-inspiring, just and merciful, you alone are kind and loving. By the co-working of the Holy Spirit, you prepared the Blessed Virgin Mary to become the mother of your Son. Receive the sacrifice of the repentant heart and the sincere desire of your servant, N., who humbly asks you for her welfare and for the welfare of the child which you permitted her to conceive. Guard the work which is yours and defend it from all the deceit and harm of our bitter enemy, so that the hand of your mercy may assist her delivery, and her child may come to the light of day without harm to serve you always in all things. Through Christ Our Lord.

All: Amen

(Here the presider sprinkles the women with holy water.)

Leader: God has given the angels charge over you
All: To keep you in all your ways.
Leader: Visit, O God, this house and drive far from it and from this your servant, N., the enemy with all his agents. May your holy angels dwell here to keep her and her child in peace, and may your blessing be always upon her.
All: Amen.

REFERENCES

Collectio Rituum. Pro Dioecesibus Civitatum Foederatarum Americae Septentrionalis. Collegeville, Minnesota: The Liturgical Press, 1964.

Eboussi Boulaga, F. *Christianity Without Fetishes: An African Critique and Recapture of Christianity.* Maryknoll, New York: Orbis Books, 1984.

Floro, Angel. *The Rites of Passage and Their Christian Values.* Kampala, Uganda: Unpublished Pastoral Studies, 1971.

Lwakale, Celestin Mubenganyi. *Sacramentalisme Chrétien et Christian-isation en Profondeur.* Rome: Gregorian University Press, 1966.

Mbiti, John S. *African Religions and Philosophy.* London: Heinemann Education Books Ltd., 1983.

Nasimiyu, Sister Anne. *Vatican II: The Problem of Inculturation.* Ph.D. Thesis. Michigan: University Microfilms International, 1987.

Parrinder, Geoffrey. *African Traditional Religion.* 3d ed. London and New York: Harper and Row, 1976.

Van Gennep, Arnold. *Rites of Passage.* Chicago: University of Chicago Press, 1960.

Wagner, Gunter. *The Bantu of Western Kenya with Special Reference to the Vugusu and Logoli.* Vol. 1. London: International African Institute, Oxford University Press, 1970.

4

The Christian Widow in African Culture

Daisy N. Nwachuku

INTRODUCTION

The Christian woman in the contemporary world is culturally and socially an endangered species. In developing nations such as those in Africa, her plight is compounded by a transitional society's tenacious hold to traditional norms while it grapples with the social changes of intruding foreign cultures. Most human societies are "patriarchal." Consequently, societal norms and sex-role functions are prescribed by the dominant, male sex. Since social cohesiveness is maintained by strict adherence to social roles, appropriate role performance usually earns approval while inappropriate performance brings disapproval, rejection, role sanction, and, in extreme cases, social ostracism. Consequently, the subordinate, female sex in transformed or transitional societies, when faced with matters of choice or preference, is bound to come into conflict with the mainstream cultural norm in question. When they lead to a so-called deviation

Daisy N. Nwachuku, a Nigerian, is Senior Lecturer in the Department of Educational Foundation and Administration of the University of Calabar, Nigeria. She is a counseling psychologist and pastoral counselor with a doctorate from Columbia University in New York.

from the norm, such cultural conflicts are normally unwelcome, whether they are based on empirical facts, emotions, or faith. This is the situation with the contemporary African Christian in a rapidly modernizing world. When an act of cultural deviation involves women's issues and thus the culturally "subordinate" sex, the role conflicts are escalated.

Another root of these role conflicts is that in traditional societies religion and culture are inseparable. The centrality of human life and of all daily activities is embedded in the people's religion. Through ancestral worship, the mediation of departed patriarchs is solicited to appease the anger of the gods or receive favors and blessings. Thus any infringement on this process of life preservation and prosperity meets with vehement resistance. In this perspective, the dilemma faced by the Christian widow in an African ritualistic but contemporary culture is highlighted.

The problem that I have investigated is: How does a contemporary African Christian woman who has been widowed practice her faith vis-à-vis the culturally prescribed burial and mourning rituals? For a clearer crystallization of the problem, I have paid attention to the following questions as well:

1. What is the African traditional concept of widowhood?
2. What burial and mourning rituals are prescribed for the widow, and which of the norms are in direct conflict with Christian practice?
3. What should be the Christian woman's response to the prescribed norms, especially in cases of conflicts and dilemmas, bearing in mind the future of her faith, her home, and her children (if any)?
4. What is the contemporary church's response to the problem in real-life situations, and is there room for improvement?

REVIEW OF RELATED LITERATURE

In preparing this essay, I discovered an upsurge of volumes, articles, and research reports on African theology in the past two decades. These documents and definitions express different concepts of what African theology is or ought to be, fears and doubts of what it might turn out to be in the distant future, and scepticism on what it can offer or whether it can favorably compete with Western theology. In the midst of this intellectual exercise, however, very little focus was found in written African theological reflections on women in a real-life African context. I do not intend here to enter into the current academic debate of what African theology is, its proper nomenclature, and whether it can compete favorably with Western theology. Rather, I accept Mbiti's (83–84) conclusion on the controversy, in which he states:

> I will use the term "African theology" . . . without apology or embarrassment, to mean theological reflection and expression by African Christians. . . . There are three main main areas of African theology today: written theology, oral theology and symbolic theology. Written African theology is the privilege of a few Christians who have had considerable education and who generally articulate their theological reflection in articles and (so far, few) books, mostly in English, French, German or other European languages. Oral theology is produced in the fields, by the masses, through song, sermon, teaching, prayer, conversation, etc. It is theology in the open air, often unrecorded, often heard only by small groups, and generally lost to libraries and seminars. Symbolic theology is expressed through art, sculpture, drama, symbols, rituals, dance, colours, numbers, etc.

In this essay on the African Christian widow I will focus on symbolic theology as expressed through symbols and rituals in burial ceremonies.

Webster's Unabridged Dictionary defines ritual as a "set form or system of rites, religious or otherwise; or the observance of a set form of rites, as in public worship."

Likewise, the same volume defines symbol as "a token, pledge, a sign by which one infers a thing, something that stands for or represents another thing; especially, an object used to represent something abstract and in theology, an abstract or compendium, creed or summary of the articles of religion." Thus, the process through which an African woman passes during the period of burial and mourning for a lost spouse involves a ritual of a traditional African religion within the social milieu in question. It is evident that some of the traditional ritualistic processes and practices have their merits and positive effects, while some others, when examined in the light of mental and physical health risks as well as in their psychosocial implications, are found to have profound negative effects on the adherents. Yet these traditions have become resistant to contemporary social changes as a result of habit, fear, or wanton insistence on known patterns for the maintenance of tribal or ethnic identity, social cohesion, and the established status quo. Challenging the insistence on continuing the negative traditional status quo, a female health researcher (Adebajo, 2) recently noted:

> It is an established fact that the more severe the effect of any harmful traditional practices are, the more likely it is that the victim will be either women or children. Men have generally been involved in the less severe forms of traditional practices.

Although the strength of Adebajo's assertion is mitigated by the fact that the culture also imposes stringent sanctions on males too (for example, sanctions against stealing), what the author wants to emphasize is sexist oppression, often accompanied by prejudice, stigmatization, and stereotyping by the stronger sex over the weaker sex, which still persists today in most societies, whether industrialized or traditional, Christian or secular.

The process of ritualistic expressions and symbolisms are the essential elements for ordering individual survival and security and the life of the society. The in-built worship embedded in ritualism and symbolism provides the internal locus of control and governs the people's total life and activities. In this regard, Uka asserts:

> Religion is a reality in human experience and pervades through life. It describes man's relationship with the supernatural world or the Ultimate Reality, generally referred to as God. This relationship finds expression in beliefs,

worship, creeds and symbols . . . Throughout history, therefore, a religion is known to be the basis of the identity of
a tribe, a nation and a community. This religious identity
has been the foundation of the separation of each from
the other and the cause of inter-group conflict.

Olford, agreeing, declares the human race to be incurably
religious, with objects of worship that range from material things
such as money and property to natural phenomena, carved
images, and ultimately the Supreme God. "Therefore, there is
no atheism because man must worship something, somehow,"
says Olford. On the African scene, Mbiti states that "most Africans do not see any contradiction in holding a mixture of beliefs
and practices." Thus he maintains that religious pluralism is
bound to exist, even in the presence of a teeming population of
African Christians.

On the contrary, Oduyoye (109) argues that religious pluralism is not only an African phenomenon but a global occurrence.
She further asserts that the presence of self-styled atheists and
humanists testifies to the secularization taking place in Africa,
and thereby refutes the popular assumption that Africans are
"notoriously" or "incurably" religious. Oduyoye's argument
could be contradicted by the positions taken by Uka and Olford
that the human person endemically seeks to worship something.
If the object of one's worship is not something outside oneself,
then it will be oneself (humanism). Therefore, the humanist has
a religion.

However, it is the combination of factors from all these theses
that form the central focus of my essay. Oduyoye (109) states:

> There is also a group that we may refer to as "tradition-
> alists." Some of these are simply theorists, but there are
> masses of people in Africa who hold to the traditional
> religious beliefs and practices of their forebearers to the
> exclusion of the missionary religions. Their religious cus-
> toms blend with their social life and are at the base of all
> their institutions and festive celebrations. It is their relig-
> ious beliefs and practices that we designate as "African."

Oduyoye categorically claims that the so-called "traditionalists" practice their African religion outside the Christian church, while Mbiti concludes that even these "traditionalists" attend church and yet comfortably hold a mixture of beliefs and practices without seeing any contradictions. Indeed, this study focuses on the issue of the apparent conflict of faith in matters requiring a clear-cut decision. For example, within the context of burial and mourning ceremonies for a deceased husband, are the traditional widowhood rituals practiced exclusively outside the actual Christian fold, or is Mbiti's claim of pluralism of faith a reality? Is the reality of conflict of faiths denied, ignored, or addressed by the contemporary African church and its theology? What church discipline does a widow face who complies with the traditional rituals as a social strategy for survival? Or, what social sanctions does a Christian woman face among her kinsmen when she resists or challenges the rituals to preserve her faith?

In defense of the contribution of African religious values to Christianity, Oduyoye (109–110) concludes:

Modernization has had a disruptive and weakening effect on African life and thus on African religion. At the same time it is evident that the missionary religions together with modern technology have proved inadequate to our needs. Since the old appears unable to stand on its own and the new by itself is proving inadequate, we should expect some creative syncretism to develop in Africa. A living Christian faith in Africa cannot but interact with African culture. In fact, there is being developed an interpretation of Christianity and specifically for Christian theology that one may describe as African.

While agreeing that a missionary religion is bound to interact with the host culture, the real-life question that we must now face is: Has the new actually proved inadequate? Is it evidently clear that the old cannot stand? Is there an agreement for a merger? Or, is there a need for a different mode of re-engagement vis-à-vis rituals and symbols? And what further role has the Christian church in Africa to play in this process of evolution?

In view of the fact that no one single piece of research can address all the areas in which traditional African life interacts with the Christian religion, I specifically limited my study to investigating rituals and symbols which a Christian woman faces at the burial and mourning ceremonies for her dead husband within the Nigerian context and in the real-life experience of some ethnic groups. I am aware of the thousands of ethnic groups in Nigeria and in Africa as a whole and the many cultural variations even in the widowhood rituals. Therefore, conclusions are restricted to my data and generalizations are only relevant to subjects similar to the sample of my study.

This essay is based on a study carried out in a clinical model with the help of four field research assistants. In-depth interviews, participant and unobtrusive observation, case-study analysis, and questionnaire techniques provide the material analyzed below.

A total of one hundred subjects were randomly selected from eighteen ethnic groupings located in seven states of the Nigerian federation. Forty of the subjects were widows. They were interviewed on the basis of the following open-ended questions:

1. How is the widow perceived at the time of her husband's death? after some years? and how is she generally treated?

2. What burial and mourning rituals is she made to go through?

3. Has she any rights to her own and family possessions?

4. In recent times, have any of the norms been refused or challenged, and on what grounds?

5. What is the current church reaction to the rituals and general treatment of the widows?

DISCUSSION

These vital research questions were posed in investigating the problems of African Christian widows. The responses present a concise summary of the emotional, spiritual, and psychosocial states in which an African widow is found among the eighteen ethnic groups studied in Nigeria. Generally, although the widow is perceived as someone to be pitied, sympathized with, and helped, she suffers emotional and spiritual violence. The widow is perceived as taboo to living husbands and other males. She is subject to hopelessness, punishment, neglect, contempt, suspicion about her treachery, or lack of good care. She is perceived as threatening to other couples' relationships and suspected of adulterous living. The result is that a widow is usually a neglected and deserted lonely woman. These perceptions of widowhood become strategies of emotional and spiritual violence.

The majority of the female subjects (78%) agreed that the African widow is still generally badly treated in the rituals. The close proportion of males who say yes to general good treatment (57%) to males who say no (43%) indicates that even the males themselves who are the proponents of the norms and rituals are aware of the adverse effects of the ceremonies on the females. In response to Question 1, the African cultural concept of widowhood as shown by data in this study is retrogressive in that it generates and encourages abuse of human dignity through widow stereotyping and stigmatization, and also through perpetuating further psychological violence to a person who is already grief-stricken at the loss of a dear spouse.

In response to Question 2 on whether any rituals are presently applied to a Christian widow, participants itemized forty-two observances. With the exception of head-shaving, all the other listed rituals are enslaving rather than liberating physically, emotionally, or spiritually. Asked if the male Christians and non-Christians observed a corresponding set of rituals at the loss of a spouse, opinions from subjects varied greatly, ranging from none to simple head-shaving, and a mourning period in which no remarriage may take place from three months to one year, depending on the man's discretion.

Generally, the subjects all agreed that the males observe no clothing, eating, or weeping rituals, nor are they subjected to any movement restrictions. Among some ethnic groups, in the case of the death of a barren wife, signs of mourning disappear soon after the burial. Data indicated further enslavement of a widow through financial and property disposition by male relatives of the deceased. About 35% of the forty widows interviewed had already resisted this practice. With the exception of three subjects (5%) who are adherents of African traditional religion, 95% of the sixty subjects agreed that in contemporary times, the widow has a right as a person to choose or resist any imposed rituals. About 83% of the respondents indicated that the churches currently resist the ritualistic mourning procedures, while 58% agreed that the church has currently assumed responsibility for the performance of the mourning ceremonies and has toned them down to lighten the burden on the widow. Thus, Question 4 on a widow's action in the face of a dilemma and Question 5 on the church's reaction were answered.

This study shows that the present state of widowhood raises some major social and theological issues of concern for both males and females in contemporary Africa.

MEANING OF MOURNING SYMBOLS AND RITUALS TO THE PEOPLE

If symbols are a compendium of articles of religion or an abstraction of a creed, and if rituals are a set form of rites as in public worship, then an infringement on either the symbols or rituals threatens a disorganization of the status quo of a people. The well-known social cohesion is endangered. Furthermore, in agreement, Mbiti, as mentioned earlier, noted that through symbolic theology, a people express their act of religious worship. Perhaps it is within this context that Oduyoye noted that modernization has had a disruptive and weakening effect on African religion, while Achebe, looking at the weakened social cohesiveness, commented that things have fallen apart and the center cannot hold.

However, if freedom of worship is a fundamental human right, the question that arises is: Has the contemporary African woman no right to choose a form of worship suitable to her spiritual well-being, whether traditionalist or a missionary religion? In Africa, the argument has always been that traditionally every member of the society is born into the family religion. But since the advent of the missionary religions, traditionalists have

Abandon or reappropriate?

been known to choose to abandon their faith for conversion to Christianity or Islam.

A second major issue of concern arising from this dilemma is that if liberation and freedom culminating in the worshiper's ultimate salvation is a basic theological concept, should the African woman who first observed the traditional religion but later chose Christianity be forced retrogressively into bondages she renounced? This is what complying with rituals of mourning — such as walking about dejected for one year, wailing, rolling on the bare floor to show grief, sleeping on floor mats when she already has a bed, and observing unhygienic meal and bath requirements — means. In addition, demands for shrine sacrifices, of which her new religion offers a viable alternative, compel her to disobey the spiritual discipline of her chosen religion.

Le Roi Jones (117), arguing for black power, noted:

> The task for Black Theology, then, is to analyze the Black person's condition in the light of God's revelation in Jesus Christ with the purpose of creating a new understanding of Black dignity among Black people, and providing the necessary soul in that people, to destroy White racism.

Within the context of liberation theology, one might ask whether cultural inhumanity in the form of religious sexism, prejudices, stigmatization, and stereotyping should be enthroned when the white racism that sought to suppress African culture is dethroned.

When the one hundred subjects were asked whether any cultural prescriptions existed for widowers, the responses ranged from none to a one-year restriction on remarriage. There were no required rituals. Thus the leniency accorded males exposes the fundamental sexism, suppression, and oppression which lie at the root of a widow's torture. Whether racist or sexist, any negative values imposed on a human life are an abuse of human dignity and a denial of human rights. Even in the context of liberation theology, African theology as an advocate for African traditional religion has no convincing answer yet to the continuation of contemporary Christian widow oppression.

Another liberation theologian, James Cone (1970: 127–28), noted:

> The interpretation of salvation as liberation from bondage is certainly consistent with the biblical view. He who needs salvation is one who has been threatened or oppressed, and his salvation consists in deliverance from danger and tyranny or rescue from imminent peril (1 Sam. 4:3; 7:8; 9:16) . . . In Israel, God is the Savior par excellence. Beginning with the Exodus, God's righteousness is for those who are weak and helpless. "The mighty work of God, in which his righteousness is manifested, is in saving the humble . . . the poor and the dispirited." The same is true in the New Testament. Salvation is release from slavery and admission to freedom (Galatians 5:1, 2 Corinthians 3:17), saying no to the fear of principalities and yes to the powers of liberty (1 John 4:18). This is not to deny that salvation is a future reality; but it is also hope that focuses on the present.

African Christian theology, while seeking to contextualize Christianity within the African milieu, must seek to minister effectively to the widow as a "total person" and to her children. When a religious custom jeopardizes the full human development of a total person and impedes progress, as exemplified in normative ritual prescriptions for the widow, a continuation of that ritual is questionable in modern times.

Indeed, based on the New Testament concept of salvation that says, "if the Son therefore shall make you free, ye shall be free indeed" (John 8:36), and, "So if anyone is in Christ, there is a new creation: old things are passed away; behold, all things are become new" (2 Cor. 5:17), enforcing upon a Christian widow rituals that compel her to regress to the things from which she has been freed (shrine sacrifice or observances to ward off premature death) is a cultural oppression that does great psychological and spiritual violence to her. By the same token, imposing any such traditional oppressive practices under the auspices of the Christian church is tantamount to putting old wine in a new skin, and conflict is bound to occur. This is a call to the church to reexamine its stand on the acceptance of some of the rituals, a reexamination that must come under the full searchlight of the death and resurrection of Jesus Christ.

THE FEMALE VOICELESSNESS IN AFRICAN RITUALISM

The male prerogative in the prescription of gender role differentiation in societies is a factor that has come under review in recent times in the light of social changes. Although there are a few occasions where female priests and prophets play active parts in the African traditional religion, in the majority of ceremonies the female presence is mere tokenry in the midst of male dominance. The current wave of women's movements, either as support, research, or pressure groups, has brought a social awareness through which female voices are becoming audible in areas hitherto tabooed. Sex-role function in rituals is one such area. A historical analysis of the origin of human societies reveals that the stringent cultural prescriptions for women were in most cases made to maintain the purity of the family tree and ensure submission and respect in the home. Women were never allowed (and are still not allowed) the opportunity to share in many policy decisions that affect them, nor may they participate fully as chief celebrants of the religious aspects of such policies. For example, Oduyoye (112) writes: "African women have a traditional belief in the benefit of sacrifice for the community . . . But I have difficulty in understanding why it is the prerogative of only one sex to sacrifice for the well-being of the community." In a religious celebration in which women are observers rather than active participants, female voicelessness continues to encourage the perpetuation of rites and rituals that foster female oppression. The fact that health hazards and risks to personality growth and development among widows have gone on unchallenged for a long period is only an accident of history. If African women are "people," they must have a chance to express their satisfaction or dissatisfaction, even in the cultic aspects of tradition that drastically affect their lives and that of their children.

FEMALE COLLABORATION WITH MALE OPPRESSORS

While in a patriarchal society males are often accused by females of being the oppressors, a counterargument often put forward by men is that some of the obnoxious and repressive role functions of women, whether in religion or in social matters, were formulated in the distant past by powerful elderly women for the purposes of female discipline in the areas of wifely submission, chastity, good maternal care, and for maintaining the aura of femininity. Concerning the treatment of widows, the argument also runs that most of these role functions even today are monitored and deviants punished by a female pressure group widely known as "daughters of the land." In some cases, they are joined by another female pressure group called the "co-wives" of the kindred who make demands and taunt the widow. These tauntings are aimed at getting the widow angry, so that she incurs a heavy fine or penalties or draws further accusations upon herself. The issue of female oppression by females in traditional Africa is an area that calls for further and immediate in-depth study as a vital contribution to the global improvement of the condition of women.

THE CHURCHES' RESPONSE TO RITUALISTIC WIDOWHOOD – A COMPROMISE, SYNCRETISM, OR SOLUTION?

About 83% of the subjects of this study indicated that the churches resist the performance of widowhood rituals, while 58% indicate a complete takeover of some selected rites by the churches and their performance within the church setting.

Here lies the source of the present African Christian faith dilemma. The question is: Should the local celebration of widowhood rituals be christianized by the church? How far does the church condone, worsen, abate, or fully participate in enhancing the cultural practices, and what are the biblical bases of the selected traditional practices if they are introduced into Christianity? Whereas data show that the church does not support oppression, the question arises as to whether the taking over of some of the rituals is an act of compromise or syncretism, or a solution.

For instance, the list of food items demanded from the widow during the night vigil or Christian wake, especially in rural areas, the items prescribed to be officially presented to the church choirs and other officials for conducting the church burial, are all issues of concern that throw the widow into limbo as to whether to lean toward the traditional or towards the church. Her choice depends on which group makes lesser demands on her and her children. Much argument can be built to support any of these positions. For example, from a fundamentalist viewpoint, the action of the churches in Africa could be seen as a compromise of faiths. In effect, some of the rituals are a continuation of African traditional beliefs. Such is the significance of head-shaving. But from a more liberal viewpoint, the churches' response fits into Mbiti's theory of religious pluralism or Oduyoye's call for creative syncretism in the African theological context.

For those who hold a strict Africanist viewpoint and for those uncompromisingly Christian fundamentalists, the issue of concern in this essay is not whether the church is going African or Western. Rather, the question is how helpful are some of the ceremonies to the emotional adjustment and rehabilitation of the widow? Do these rituals have any positive effects — for example, the social competition for the most expensive coffin or the most sophisticated grave, the emotional torture of keeping the corpses too long while scouting for money to afford the ostentatious entertainments associated with traditional burial, while exorbitant bills are run up in the mortuary? Of course, the church's sanction of shaving, wearing mourning clothes, the ceremonial removal of mourning clothes, and yearly ceremonial remembrances are issues that need to be reexamined. In them, traditional ritualism overlaps with Old Testament practices. For example, in Leviticus 19:27–28, shaving, tattooing and such during mourning were sure signs of idol worship, unbelief, and superstition and were biblically condemned. If we in modern times tenaciously cling to them even within the cultic processes of the church out of concern for being truly African, of what use are these practices to the widow and her household, especially if her children are at a tender age, or if she is widowed at an old age?

While agreeing that an African should be a Christian within his or her social milieu, a more serious issue facing African Christians, and to which African theologians must address themselves, is: What are the biblical bases for some of the rituals that go with widowhood, and on what basis have they been incorporated into the practices of some Christian churches in the light of the gospel and especially of the finality of death and the resurrection of Jesus? In this respect, I refer specifically to head-shaving, the period of confinement, the wearing of specific mourning clothes (white, black, or colored), the second burial or memorial services, specified mourning periods and mourning patterns, burial entertainments and heavy burial expenses, the Christian unveiling of tombstones, the yearly remembrances of the dead in ceremonial mourning styles, and so forth.

In the light of 1 Thessalonians 4:13–18, must the widow ceremonially wail and weep according to pattern? Must she shave? Are these not to be left to personal choice, as the bereaved feels? For example, Joseph mourned for his father in Canaan for seven days (Gen. 50:10), while the whole of Israel mourned for Moses for thirty days (Deut. 34:8). The New Testament is silent on some of these issues, but it is believed that the practices persist in Africa because the present-day church acquired them from pagan Greek, Roman, and European cultural traditions. It seems however that social changes have caused many of them to have been abandoned in Western culture. Does the continued observance of some of these practices make the African Christian more Christian even in the midst of increasing resistance by widows, as shown by 34% of the forty widows interviewed? This area calls for further research and proper documentation with larger samples of Christian widows in many more African nations and many more denominations, and among many more ethnic groups.

THE SPIRITUAL AND PHYSICAL REHABILITATION OF THE WIDOW WITHIN THE CHURCH

On an even more serious note of conflict, if the African church toes the line of condonation or compromise, who then helps the widow to handle the fierce opposition she faces from her kin when she opts to exercise her freedom of mourning choice and freedom of worship? How does the widow handle the problems of social and psychological rehabilitation that go with the traditionalist view, such as her dispossession from the family finances, land, and property, which is the prevalent practice today? Among the eighteen ethnic groups interviewed, only one group has a tradition which allows the widow to inherit family property. That is to say, in most traditional African societies, the customary norms have no law of inheritance for the widow.

Although the church has intervened to take over some rituals in order to forestall abuse, the African Christian widow still remains handicapped in terms of finance and property inheritance. If the widow is not in paid employment or has no means of steady income, she is thrown into penury, which goes against Christian principles. In this respect, the church appears to be helplessly silent. In African traditional practice neither the Christian nor the non-Christian widow has any legal property rights, no legal protection against violence or against being ejected from the marital home if she refuses to enter into a levirate marriage (i.e., to marry her deceased husband's brother). Social stigmatization, stereotyping, and sexual harassments bordering on assaults from neighborhood men are often rampant.

Facts like these present real-life challenges to the contemporary church and to African theology. The voiceless Christian widow and her children call loudly and clearly to the church for rescue. True religion must minister to the whole being — body, soul, and spirit — and it is the Word of God, as embodied in the life and teachings of Christ, which provides the foundation for this ongoing task.

"Ultimate and absolute authority in matters of faith can and must reside only in the Word of God, who was made flesh, died and rose again for our salvation, and abides forever in His church" (Flew and Davis). The precepts of Jesus Christ, who himself said, "I am the Way, the Truth and the Life" (John 14:6) and "Behold, I make all things new" (Rev. 21:5), should be the impetus that spurs African Christian scholars to seek strategies for a renewal unto new life and new hope found only in God for the widow who has been grief-stricken by the death of her spouse. Thus is theology translated from abstraction into reality.

IMPLICATIONS FOR PASTORAL COUNSELING

Results of this study show that there are many issues in the present lives of African Christian widows that clearly call for pastoral counseling as an essential service from the church. Properly organized counseling sessions are needed in which the widow is taught to appraise her new situation realistically and is equipped with new skills in order to avoid being disappointed by having undue expectations of the community members. She needs to be counseled on property ownership and new occupational adjustments, so that she can assume her new responsibility as the family's sole bread winner. The widow also needs help in acquiring strategies for handling grief without getting hopelessly broken. She needs strategies for handling loneliness and desertion, and techniques for decision-making in her new role of leadership for herself and the family. She also needs negotiation skills so that she can communicate her dissatisfaction and ask for a change. The therapy sessions within the church's counseling ministry provide the widow with an opportunity to reevaluate herself as a real person and not as someone with a social stigma or taboo. In this sense, group therapy sessions will provide a viable psychological support and a solidarity base for resisting those areas in which the deliverance of widows from bondage is still most predominantly unchallenged. These sessions will help the churches to provide full solidarity with the widow during the period of her transition into her new situation.

The concept of caring in the African extended family should enhance the pastoral caring ministry within the African church in a much more pronounced way than in the Western world. The biblical injunction of James 1:27 should spur a thriving ministry of visitation with gifts, prayers, and other helps to the widow far more than the occasional visits made to them on specific feast days during the year. Ideally, the biblical concept of levirate marriage or "widow-inheritance" in African culture was meant to serve the purpose of caring and security in a particular setting and carried with it an element of personal choice. But the traditional African concept of wife-inheritance, pushed to its extreme by human greed, leads to forced cohabitation of the widow with a selected kinsman of the husband. If she refuses, she risks being ousted from the matrimonial compound or being forced to repay her dowry in order to earn her independence. This is the case among some ethnic groups. The New Testament injunction of 1 Timothy 5:9–14, if followed by the church in its pastoral ministry, provides a molested widow with a refuge and an emotional support in defense of her faith and her action. Unfortunately, the church and its African theology has remained uncomfortably ambivalent in this aspect for too long, leaving the widow alone and torn between tradition and Christianity.

Professing African Christians and scholars should take a cue from our Lord Jesus. This is where our faith should be anchored, even while we strive as Africans to protect our traditions. Ngumoha asked a passionate question in a church synod: "Who will deliver the bereaved from local celebrations of culture?" In response, he turned to the church to offer deliverance. Must the widow continue to lament publicly over her dead husband for years? Who will minister to her shame- and guilt-ridden spirit for failing to meet the social and financial exhibitions of grief and sorrow? Who will reach down to her inner being which aches from the demands of living up to expectations? We believe that African women theologians can rise to give the church a good reminder and assistance.

CONCLUSION

I conclude this study by stating that the African Christian widow is a "person," whole and worthy of dignity despite her grief-stricken situation. If she is left to continue being torn apart by two worlds — traditionalists and Christianity — she is abandoned to suffer cultural and cultic oppressions. Further, although social life in modern Africa is still intricately tied up with traditional beliefs, a majority of present-day Africans, literate or not, adhere to the Christian faith, either as ardent believers and active participants or as interested affiliate members of some churches. There is today a great deal of ambivalence or dualism among many African Christians when issues touch on life-threatening traditional beliefs or superstitions; this explains the continued ritualistic treatment of the widow even when she is a Christian. In my observation, the church's approach to this issue, even in the present decade and in many denominations, is an ongoing evolution of her strategies toward an improved life for widows. At present, the church needs more encouragement rather than destructive criticism or antagonism, and we encourage the church to be more sensitive to her observers and critics in this exercise.

The church needs to take a firm stand to expunge obnoxious anti-Christian traditions and rituals. This stand must translate theories and rhetoric into practical action as daily challenges occur. Traditionalism needs to condemn dehumanization.

Let me conclude by noting, with neither pretence nor embarrassment, that in our technological era blind adherence to those cultic traditions that impede full human intellectual, moral, spiritual, emotional, and social development, and that are inspired by sexism or any other negative values, is a retrogressive step into human oppression and bondage. Yet, a total condemnation of any form of worship because it is traditional is immature as well as irrational. True African Christianity must seek a healthy "inner" renewal to energize the spirit into improving the quality of life for humanity in general and for the oppressed, such as the widow, in particular. Although I admit that one major limitation of this study is that eighteen ethnic groups are not a global representative of African culture, and that even within the same culture there are still variations, the main thrust of my thesis is that widows are suppressed as people in one form or another in every African society because of the traditional religious beliefs and cultural and sociological practices that have a tremendous influence on every aspect of African life, including the lives of Christians.

Paul's first Letter to Timothy (5:1–14), which clearly states the New Testament church's attitude toward widows, should guide every African Christian community. Salvation of humanity was the whole essence of Christ's earthly ministry. He lived and preached deliverance to those in bondage and freedom to those captive in body, soul, and spirit. Similarly, if the oppressed widow is delivered from her bondage, the Christian concept of salvation in Jesus Christ will be transformed from faith as a religious abstraction to faith in action. True African theology must seek to reinstate the woman, as Jesus Christ did, into her full status as a "total person," whole and worthy, a being created in the image of God, and a fully accepted member of the Body of Christ.

REFERENCES

Achebe, Chinua. *Things Fall Apart.* Greenwich, Connecticut: Fawatt, 1959.

Adebajo, C. O. "Female Circumcision and Other Dangerous Practices to Maternal Health in Nigeria." Paper presented at the Women's Health Research Network Seminar and Special Panel at the Society of Gynaecology and Obstetrics of Nigeria Conference, Calabar, September 1989.

Cone, J. H. *Black Theology & Black Power.* New York: The Seabury Press, 1969.

Cone, J. H. *A Black Theology of Liberation.* New York: Orbis Books, 1990.

Mbiti, J. "The Biblical Basis for Present Trends in African Theology." In K. Appiah-Kubi and S. Torres, eds. *African Theology en Route,* 83–94. New York: Orbis Books, 1979.

Ngumoha, I. B. "Who Will Deliver the Bereaved from Local Celebrations of Culture?" The Second Motion of the Second Session of the Sixth Synod of the Anglican Diocese of Aba, Abayi-Umuocham, July 1989.

Oduyoye, M. A. "The Value of African Religious Beliefs and Practices for Christian Theology." In K. Appiah-Kubi and S. Torres, eds. *African Theology en Route,* 109–116. New York: Orbis Books, 1977.

Olford, S. "The Professor Who Became a Possessor: Nicodemus Who Came to Jesus by Night." Encounter: A radio message. ELWA: Liberia, September 1989.

Uka, E. M. "Is Religious Education Necessary in Contemporary Schools?" In D. N. Nwachuku, ed. *Contemporary Issues in Nigerian Education.* Enugu, 1989.

5

Paradise Lies at the Feet of Muslim Women

Rabiatu Ammah

INTRODUCTION

I am grateful for the opportunity to share my ideas on the question of women and religion. In my essay I shall focus on women in Islam, and in so doing I shall attempt to discuss the Koranic material which for Muslims is the scripture upon which faith and practice are based. After considering the ideal, we will attempt to see how the status of the Muslim woman actually works in practice. This will be done under three main headings: spiritual, legal, and social.

The Koran teaches no theological doctrines that make woman the originator of sin. It does not make Eve responsible for the fall of man. It refutes the assertion that woman was first deceived and declares in unambiguous terms that both man and woman were deceived simultaneously, and that both were forgiven after they had repented. There is no scriptural basis for

Rabiatu Ammah, a Muslim from Ghana, is active in multi-faith deliberations. She has a doctorate in Islamic Studies from the University of Birmingham, England.

the Muslim man to blame woman for the sins of humanity. Woman in Islam or woman in the Koran is not evil.

The Koran does not mention that woman was created from the rib of man. It is rather categorical and states that both man and woman have been created from the same substance:

> O mankind, reverence
> Your guardian-Lord
> Who created you
> From a single Person,
> Created of like nature
> His mate and from them twain
> Scattered (like seeds)
> Countless men and women.   (4:1)

The Koran, therefore, sees woman as an individual who possesses a soul and a personality of her own. In the sight of God, woman is completely free, and in respect of her moral and spiritual status she is equal to man, for when God instructs humankind in the Koran to worship God, both men and women are addressed. When it comes to ethical obligations and rewards, the Koran clearly states

> If any do deeds
> Of righteousness
> Be they male or female
> And have faith
> They will enter heaven
> And not the least injustice
> Will be done to them.   (4:124)

From the purely Koranic point of view, the most favored in the sight of Allah are the most pious. It does not matter what gender they are.

In the matter of legal rights, the Koran makes specifications which are guaranteed for every human being. For example, it acknowledges the right of every woman to buy and sell independently of her husband. She may enter into contracts, and earn, hold, and manage her own money and property. She is, therefore, economically independent.

In addition, the Koran grants women a share in inheritance and warns men against depriving her of that inheritance. The Koran says much regarding inheritance, and since the subject is vast, I shall concentrate on those verses related to women. The Koran says:

> Men shall have a portion
> Of what their parents
> And kindred leave, and
> Women shall have a
> Portion of what their
> Parents leave, whether
> It be little or much
> A determined portion.   (4:8)

It continues:

> God instructs you
> Concerning your children!
> For a male, the like
> Of a portion of two
> Females. And if there
> Be women, i.e. (daughters
> Above two) then let them
> Have two-thirds of what
> The deceased leaves ...   (2:12)

Again a particular portion is paid to the mother after payments of any bequests and debts have been made.

The wife is not left alone, and the Koran specifically states that she should be given a share, whether the man likes it or not:

> Half of what your wives
> Leave shall be yours,
> If they have no issues
> But if they have issues

Then a fourth of what
They leave shall be yours
After paying the bequests
They shall bequeath and debts
And your wives shall have
A fourth part of what you
Leave, if you have no issue;
But if you have issue, they
Shall have an eighth part
Of what you leave after
Paying the bequests ...   (4:13–14)

It is clear that a daughter and wife both have a share in the estate of a father/husband and vice versa. However, what is glaring is the fact that a daughter gets half of what a son is given. The reason given for this discrepancy or inequality is that a woman is provided for by the men of the household. Thus the man's double share is equitable.

Seen in the context of the pre-Islamic culture, in which women were not only deprived of inheritance but were also inherited against their will (for they were considered property), the Koranic portion considerably improved the lot of the woman. Clearly, one had to take into consideration the fact that in that culture the man was the financial backbone of the family. Consequently, women who were not by role description obliged to finance themselves were not to get the same share as their male counterparts. In the partriarchal society in which Islam was revealed, such an allocation was deemed equitable.

The question that remains concerns the industrial revolution and the changes that have taken place so that women participate fully in providing for the family. Can this inequity stand in a different context? Moreover, whether or not this allotment is respected is another thing altogether. It is probably enough to say that in certain Muslim societies, immovable property is not passed on to a woman because the property would then become part of the husband's estate if she remarries.

One other area that may be discussed is the legal right of women to give testimony and the subsequent interpretations that have been given to the Koranic verse which reads:

> And get two witnesses out of your men. Then a man and
> two women such as you choose for witnesses so that if one
> of them errs the other can remind her. (2:282)

Obviously, in the pre-Islamic context in which public affairs were
very much left in the hands of men, women had limited insights
into such areas. The Koran was and is, therefore, emphasizing
the correctness of testimony rather than the number who gave
testimony. It is in this specifically seventh-century context that
the question of justice, which is a central value in Islam and, for
that matter, in the Koran, is brought into focus. Specific legal
procedures are beyond dispute. It follows automatically that new
laws should be formulated in harmony with the underlying universal values, so that they do justice to woman.

In the marital bond, which has been discussed here, the
Koran has assigned specific roles and obligations to both partners, not forgetting the rights that go with these responsibilities.
The Koran states that marriage is a must for Muslims. And
unless one has a very good reason for not getting involved, this
social contract has to be entered into. It is concluded between
the man and woman. The woman does not have to be forced,
and if she is forced, she has every right to repudiate it. Upon
marriage the woman was to be given a dowry, the amount of
which was settled between the husband and wife. The Koran
says:

> And give the women
> (in marriage) their dowry
> as a free gift.   (4:4)

The Koran states that the dowry was to be given to the wife,
and not to the father or relatives of the girl, as was the case in
pre-Islamic Arabia.

The woman is, therefore, considered part of the marriage
negotiations. She is subject to it, and not an object in it. In the
Koran, men and women are garments unto each other (2:187).
They have to work together, each playing their roles properly.
Before the question of roles and the issues of interpretation
regarding the essential verse in the Koran are discussed, it is

important to make one observation regarding polygamy.

Muslims are stereotyped as being polygamous, and this is one area that has to be studied within the cultural context. After being permitted an unlimited number of women in pre-Islamic times, men were limited to four by the Koran. However, the following condition applied:

> If ye fear that ye shall
> Not be able to deal justly
> With the orphans
> Marry women of your choice
> Two, or three, or four,
> But if ye fear that ye
> Shall not be able to deal
> Justly with them then only one
> Or a captive that your
> Right hand possesses.   (43)

It continues:

> Ye are never able to
> Be fair and just
> As between women
> Even if it is your
> Ardent desire
> But turn not away (from a woman)
> Altogether so as to leave her
> As it were hanging in the air.   (4:129)

Muslims would therefore argue that the trend in the Koran is toward monogamy, a situation which was not possible at that time due to the prevailing social conditions. The widely accepted practice of polygamy and the existence of the many widows and orphans left by war and therefore in need of protection through marriage militated against outlawing it properly.

The crucial question that has been asked, therefore, is: Did Islam allow this conditional polygamy as a remedy to a particular situation? And if so, is that situation still present? There is no doubt that there are disadvantages in the institution of polygamy, but can one actually stop a woman who goes and looks for a cowife for her husband? Can one put a stop to men who have extramarital affairs and second families whether the wife likes it or not? I do not know, and I do not have an answer to the question of polygamy.

Whether or not a woman is in a polygamous marriage, she is expected to function first as a mother. The role of the mother in the family institution is crucial and is sometimes underestimated by women themselves. In this role, she is considered the first educator of the child, for her knees are considered the first school of the child. Consequently, the Koranic emphasis on education and seeking knowledge is much more essential for the Muslim woman. As one who nurtures the children in the family, which is the basic unit of society, she herself has to be very educated, be it formally or informally.

Having seen the worth, value, and importance of women in this regard, the Holy Prophet is known to have said, "Paradise lies at the feet of your mothers." Again, when asked which of the two parents deserved more respect, the Prophet said, "your mother," then "your mother," then "your mother," and then "your father."

Unfortunately, the Muslim woman in many parts of Africa lacks this education and, very painfully, education about her religion and what the Koran says about her and to her. As a Ghanaian, I can give examples from my own culture. One can accept, understand, though not justify men's claims that Muslim women cannot do this and cannot do that. But how can one explain a Muslim woman sitting in a mosque and telling younger women not to come in to worship? Again, the lack of knowledge about Islam and its teachings is responsible for some customs such as female circumcision and child marriage.

In Sudan, for example, and in some parts of North Africa, there is no doubt that female circumcision is prevalent. Sadly, this female circumcision has been attributed to Islam. Furthermore, the fact that it has been called by the term "Sunna" in the Sudanese context, which is an Islamic concept, leaves much room for ambiguity. Circumcision has nothing to do with Islam. Muslim countries that practice it are practicing something that is more cultural than Koranic. Indeed, one would have to comb the whole of the Koran for a verse that remotely sounds as if it sanctions female circumcision, and such a verse would be hard to find.

Without doubt, women themselves have perpetuated the status and roles assigned them in Muslim societies for two main reasons. First there is the question of culture and its interaction with religion. Very often Islam has interacted with cultures, and sometimes, as a result, it is difficult to separate the essentials of the religion from the cultures of the people. Hence the general misconception exists that everything that happens in a Muslim society is necessarily Islamic. Clearly, Islam as set forth in the Koran abhors forced marriages and levirate marriage. Yet these take place in Muslim societies. Culture has therefore to be separated from religion, if possible, in order not to give a blurred vision of the status of woman.

The second important issue that has to be tackled is the way in which the Koran has been interpreted. It is very clear that throughout the centuries both commentators and traditional scholars have emphasized restrictive norms with the purpose of legitimizing these norms for women in Islam. One thing that is apparent from these commentaries is that the almost exclusively male interpretations of Islam have suited male interests, although interpretation of role expectations for Muslim women may vary. One factor common to all interpretations is their intention to keep the Muslim woman subordinated to role expectations. Sadly, in making these commentaries many men refuse to take into account the contextual realities regarding the verses revealed. Usually they discuss the how and not the why. For most Muslims, everything the commentators have said is sacrosanct, and there should be no asking why.

I would like to give examples by showing how interpretations have dealt with one of the most important passages in the Koran relating to women. As discussed earlier, the Koran apportions roles and rights to the man and woman. The prime duty of the woman is to nurture the children, and the man has the responsibility of providing for the family's economic needs. He is, therefore, the financial backbone of the family. Regarding this, the Koran says:

> Men are the protectors and maintainers
> Of women because God has
> Given the one more strength
> Than the other, and because
> They support them from
> Their means. (4:34)

This verse has been interpreted in such a way as to read into the Koran man's superiority over woman. For the traditional Muslim exegesis, therefore, the woman has to be obedient and submissive to the husband to the extent that he can even chastise her. This verse has been used to justify the secondary position given to woman in most Muslim societies on the basis that it is Koranic, purely and simply Islamic.

Modern Muslim scholars, however, have argued against this traditional and authoritative interpretation and manipulation of this verse. In understanding the intention of the verse, it is important to note the financial role of men as it influences their designation as guardians and protectors of women. The term is, therefore, a normative one and should be understood as such. In trying to explain why man has been given the financial role, modern Muslim scholars have stressed that in a family relationship the biological nature of a woman is such that she is the only one of the two capable of bearing children. As such, she should not be overburdened with the additional problem of sustaining them.

What is perhaps more disheartening is the methodological error to which most commentators have subjected themselves. Muslims would argue that there is a methodology of Koranic exegesis. Many things have to be taken into consideration before commentaries are made. Yet assuming that the interpretation of this is correct, it may still be argued that the commentators have made a mess and thus it is very clear that this verse cannot be taken as the Koran's final statement on the relationship between men and women. This is because, at the time of the revelation of this verse, Islamic society had not developed to its fullness.

Women who had, prior to the Koranic revelation, been treated as chattel were gradually becoming an important part of the Islamic society. One would, therefore, argue that another verse should be taken as the final statement on women. This is contained in the following passage:

> The believers men and women
> Are protectors one of another
> They enjoin what is just
> And forbid what is evil
> They observe regular prayers
> And obey Allah and His
> Apostle. On them will Allah
> Pour his mercy for Allah
> Is exulted in power and wise. (9:71)

The contention of my essay is that the Koran elevated the status of woman vis-à-vis her status during the pre-Islamic era. She was given an identity with a soul, accountable to God, punished or rewarded according to her deeds, and given property. Historical developments and cultural influences have, however, blurred the image of the Muslim woman. Her image is a stereotyped one. She has to depend psychologically, emotionally, and financially on her husband, and again she is thought of as one of four wives. Although these are stereotypes, the very fact that they are the reality cannot be disputed. Sadly, some of these stereotypes are perpetuated by Muslim women themselves.

However, the reconstruction of the image of the Muslim woman and her real life has to be done in a scholarly way. For, as a Muslim, I believe that God is a just God. Consequently, I work on the assumption that peace and justice are what God intends for the entire creation. It is in this light that I argue that, within the cultural, socioeconomic, and political systems in which the Koran was revealed, certain things might have held good. However, as times change these verses have to be reinterpreted in the light of modern developments. After all, Muslims have always claimed that the Koran and its principles are for all people and all times. Therefore, it has to be dynamic and its interpretation not static.

Yet I am not advocating that women should do it alone. The Koran urges men and women to work together to create peace and justice on earth. Further, although I have focused on Muslim women, it is my opinion that the problems faced by Muslim women in Africa and those of other African women may be only slightly different. Whether we are Muslim or Christian, we belong to an African traditional culture that influences our lives. Hence in a way, as African women, it is religion in general that affects all of us. To focus on the Koran and how its dominant interpretation accords Muslim women a low status is, in a sense, to be part of an integrated effort to focus on women and religion in Africa.

I have tried to point out that if the contextual realities at the time of the Koranic revelation are properly studied and taken into consideration, the inherent dynamic nature of Islam would be brought to the fore.

In discussing the Koranic material and critically evaluating it, my aim has been to point to the ideal as the criteria by which Muslims should judge themselves. In reality, the picture might be bleak for Muslim women, but we must also aim at the ideal. So must women in all religions.

PART 2

AFRICAN WOMEN
AND
SEXUAL PRACTICES

6

Interpreting Old Testament Polygamy through African Eyes

Musimbi R. A. Kanyoro

INTRODUCTION

Today it is quite acceptable for people to read the Bible through their own eyes and their own experiences. However, for Bible translators, the question of being faithful to the original messages, original forms, original authors and audience still presents quite difficult problems. Yet it is no secret that in reality, it is almost impossible to translate or interpret a text without coloring it, sieving it, or molding it through our own entire network of beliefs, reality, and language.

In this article, I would like to take a look at the terminology used in biblical polygamy, and to examine how Africans who read the Bible through translations into their own languages understand this terminology in relation to African polygamy. I chose this subject, because I have worked in the field of Bible

Musimbi R. A. Kanyoro, a Kenyan, is Executive Secretary for Women in Church and Society of the Lutheran World Federation. She has a doctorate in Linguistic Biblical Studies from the University of Texas, Austin.

translation and have the experience of what happens during the search for appropriate biblical terminology in various cultures.

POLYGAMY DEFINED

In its technical meaning, the term "polygamy" refers to the marrying of many wives or husbands simultaneously or marrying many times, that is, consecutive marriages. However, the practice of marrying many husbands, a form of polygamy known specifically as "polyandry," is uncommon today. Therefore, the term "polygamy" has become confused with "polygyny," which signifies a matrimonial situation in which there is one husband but two or more wives. This is a common marriage style in the world today, and seems to have been accepted and practiced by the Hebrew people. Therefore, we will be using the term "polygamy" in its popular meaning, that is, the marrying of many wives by one man.

POLYGAMY IN THE OLD TESTAMENT

Much has been written about marriage in the Old Testament. Old Testament Hebrew has no single word for marriage; however, sufficient evidence of the marriage system which may have existed has been deduced from the text of the Bible itself and from literature of parallel civilizations that existed alongside biblical cultures. Despite numerous questions that are practically unanswered by these sources, we certainly have some impression of the kind of polygamy that existed in Old Testament times. The Bible is silent in its use of the word "polygamy" or "polygyny," but it is quite explicit in showing the practice. Apart from Isaac, Abraham, and Joseph, the patriarchs were often polygamists. Jacob (Gen. 29) and Esau (Gen. 36) each had more than one wife. Even Moses, the great lawgiver had two wives, Zipporah and an Ethiopian one (Exod. 2:21, Num. 12:1). However, in these and other cases, the Hebrews seem to have made a clear distinction between wives and concubines—a distinction I would like to explore below.

WIVES

A study of various marriage situations in the Old Testament suggests that there was a formula for taking a wife or wives. Even though it is often said that the initiative for an Old Testament marriage came from the parents or their appointees, it was mainly the male members of the family or male agents who undertook that responsibility (Gen. 24). A prospective wife was chosen from the clan of the prospective husband, with a view to protecting the family's inheritance (Gen. 20:12, 24:4, 24:15, 24:29, 28:2; Num. 36:8).

In some cases, the women seem to have had some say on whether to accept being taken for wives. Rebecca was asked if she wanted to live with Isaac, and she replied in the affirmative (Gen. 24:58ff). However, we do not have any evidence as to whether Leah was consulted when Jacob decided to take her sister Rachel as her cowife. Marriage required mutual acceptance by both families, the man's and the woman's. Marriage was not complete without the paying of *mahar*, that is, the bride-price to the woman who was being married.

Before marriage, a woman did not have an independent identity. A woman was regarded as the daughter of her father. After the marriage she became the wife of her husband. Bird (p. 261) observes that "the wife's primary contribution to the family was her sexuality which was regarded as the exclusive property of her husband both in respect to its pleasure and its fruit." The law strictly forbade both premarital sex and extramarital sex. The Old Testament law even had stipulations for husbands who might be suspicious of their wives' unfaithfulness. The reverse was not an issue (Num. 5:11–31). As for the fruit of woman, the Old Testament Hebrews placed great emphasis on progeny. A large family—in particular sons—was seen as a blessing from Yahweh (Gen. 24:60, Ps. 127:3). This resulted in two forms of polygamy. The levirate laws obliged the brother of a man who died without leaving a son to take as "wife" the widow and bear sons to continue his brother's name (Deut. 25:5–10, Ruth 4:10). From another point of view, a barren woman was obliged to find a surrogate to sleep with her husband in order to produce children on her behalf. This aspect will be treated in detail later.

OTHER WAYS OF OBTAINING WIVES
AMONG THE HEBREWS

The laws did not forbid a man to have sex with a virgin; rather, they simply imposed a small fine and required the man to marry that woman (Exod. 22:16). This definitely resulted in more instances of polygamy. If a man raped a girl, he was only required to pay the bride-price and take the girl as his wife, and never to divorce her as long as he lived (Deut. 22:29). Some see these laws as protection for women, but others see little protection to be admired in them. It is argued that they were simply social codes made by men that favored men's interests.

The Book of Judges presents other ways in which men acquired wives:

> Then they thought, "The yearly festival of the LORD at Shiloh is coming soon." (Shiloh is north of Bethel, south of Lebonah, and east of the road between Bethel and Shechem.) They said to the Benjaminites, "Go and hide in the vineyards and watch. When the girls of Shiloh come out to dance during the festival, you come out of the vineyards. Each of you take a wife by force from among the girls and take her back to the territory of Benjamin with you. If their fathers or brothers come to you and protest, you can say, 'Please let us keep them, because we did not take them from you in battle to be our wives. And since you did not give them to us, you are not guilty of breaking your promise.'" The Benjaminites did this; each of them chose a wife from the girls who were dancing in Shiloh and carried her away. Then they went back to their own territory, rebuilt their towns, and lived there. (Judg. 21:19–23)

During the time of the judges, polygamy seems to have been very widespread. Some of the judges were super-polygamists. It is said of Gideon that "he had seventy sons, because he had many wives. He also had a concubine in Shechem: she bore him a son and he named him Abimelech" (Judg. 8:30–31). Ibzan of Bethlehem is mentioned only for his thirty sons and thirty daughters (Judg. 12:9). We presume they were children of several mothers. The same can be said of a man named Abdon who "had forty sons and thirty grandsons, who rode on seventy donkeys" (Judg. 12:14)! In all these cases and many others, we hear nothing of the methods they used to procure these wives and concubines. For example, when women war captives were taken as wives and concubines (Judg. 5:30), how was it determined who was to be a wife or who to be a concubine? What distinguished a wife from a concubine is still a mystery.

The period of the Hebrew monarchy was characterized by large harems. An interesting factor here is that the wives could be taken freely from outside the tribe. In the time of the patriarchs and some of the judges, endogamy was the norm. In the monarchical period, we find not only political marriages such as that of Solomon and the Pharaoh's daughter (1 King. 9:16), but also Jewish women marrying non-Jewish men (2 Sam. 12:8). In the earlier period, it seems that only wives inherited. All along I have alluded to concubines being acquired in the same way as wives; I will now take a detailed look at the concept of Old Testament concubinage.

CONCUBINES

The Hebrew word usually translated as concubine is *pilegesh*. Mackenzie (549) says, "The term *pilegesh* designates a woman who cohabits habitually with the same man; she does not apppear to have the rank of a wife and there is no indication that the union is permanent." This definition does not tell us exactly whether it is the cohabitation, legality, or permanence, or some or all of these which made a woman *pilegesh*. However, quite a large number of references are made to *pilegesh* by the Old Testament writers. This indicates that concubinage existed in the Old Testament, as an institution regulated by custom and, to some extent, by law.

Young's Analytical Concordance (195) defines a concubine as a "half-wife." The *Good News Concordance* (GNC) defines it as "a servant woman who, although not a wife, had sexual relations with her master. She had important legal rights and her master was referred to as husband" (197). Both these definitions present a problem of interpretation and consequently of translation. With tongue in cheek, one may ask of Young, which half is wife? The GNC definition is helpful but confusing among polygamous people. If the master is to be referred to as husband, then it would follow that the servant girl is a wife!

Indeed, from the data available it is not possible to be completely certain of the legal rights of concubines as individuals, especially the non-Jewish concubines as is alleged by the GNC definition. In some instances, it appears that the sons of concubines had inheritance rights and could be regarded as having the same status as the sons of the wives (Gen. 35:23–26). Yet in most cases, they seem to have taken second place both in their treatment and in inheritance (Gen. 21:10, 25:5–6; cf. Judg. 11:1–2). *Harper's Bible Dictionary* comments on this issue: "Perhaps the right of the sons of a concubine to inherit was dependent upon the wishes of his father. This would accord well with the laws of Hammurabi Code (170–71), which stated that if a father legally recognized as his sons the children borne to him by a slave girl, they were to be counted among his heirs; but if he failed to acknowledge them, they had no claim to his estate" (*Harper's Bible Dictionary*, 422).

Hebrew slaves sold into concubinage seem to have been protected by the law (Exod. 21:7–11). However, the restrictions imposed by the law show that concubines had no rights as individuals. They could be purchased or resold, or their support removed from them, all at the whim of the man who owned them. The text of Deuteromony 21:10–14 seems to condone the making of war captives into concubines but restricts the selling of those women war captives because they had had forced intercourse with their captors. My own interpretation of this case is that it is a continuation of the guarding of the men's sexual jealousy. According to the Old Testament Hebrew thought system, a woman who has had intercourse with another man was considered defiled and unclean and must of necessity be protected from passing her defilement to "an innocent man."

Insofar as the ownership of concubines is concerned, Mackenzie comments that "the harem of the householder consisted of all his wives, and all the female slaves who were not personal property of his wives or his sons" (p. 550). While this may be generally true of harems, it seems that concubines who acted as surrogates for childless wives were the personal property of those wives. This seems to apply to the situations of Sarah and Hagar (Gen. 16:1ff), Rachel and Bilhah (Gen. 30:3), and Leah and Zilpah (Gen. 30:9). Jacob's union with his two concubines seems firmer than that of Abraham and Hagar. Jacob seems to treat all his sons with equal consideration, although not when he feels threatened. When on his return home Jacob goes to meet Esau, he fears that Esau might kill him and his family. So he places the concubines and their children in the frontline, and Rachel, his favorite wife, is placed at the rear (Gen. 33:2). However, neither Bilhah nor Zilpah is as well characterized by the biblical authors as Hagar. Concubines in the Bible generally remain caricatures. A study of Hagar in relationship to Sarah might help us to gain a bit more understanding of Hebrew concubinage. It will also show us the relationship that existed between the women themselves in the Old Testament polygamous society.

FROM HANDMAID TO A CONCUBINE: THE STORY OF HAGAR

Hagar was an Egyptian slave in the service of Sarah. The Bible does not tell us how Sarah obtained Hagar. While it is clear that the chief source of slaves was war captives (1 Kings 9:21, Num. 31:25–47, Josh. 9:23), it does not seem likely that Hagar had been a war captive. Relationships between Israel and Egypt are said to have been peaceful at that time. Moreover, Hagar was a private slave. Private slaves or their families were often debt defaulters (Exod. 22:2; 2 Kings 4:1) or people who sold themselves voluntarily (Lev. 25:39, Exod. 21:5–6, Deut. 15:16–17). Travel between Canaan and Egypt does not seem to have been a problem (Gen. 12:10ff). Based on these facts, a case has been made that Hagar was probably a poor Egyptian girl who willingly sold herself into slavery (Tamez, 7–8). She became Sarah's personal assistant or handmaid. Sarah may have acquired Hagar during their journey to Egypt (Gen. 12:10–20).

Sarah and Abraham were a rich couple who saw their riches as a special blessing from God. The Bible tells us that Sarah was not only rich but also beautiful (Gen. 12:14). The only fulfillment lacking to make her a complete matriarch was sons. Sarah was convinced that she must bear children for her master Abraham. She viewed her condition of barrenness as a curse from the Lord. The Bible puts her words as, "The Lord has kept me from having children" (Gen. 16:2). On finding that she could not bear children, Sarah resorted to a practice which seems to have been common in the Mesopotamian region. She gave Hagar, her personal slave (handmaid), to Abraham in accordance with the Hammurabi Code (144–145). The Bible says, "So she gave Hagar to him to be his concubine (Gen. 16:3). Apart from the Good News Bible and the New American Standard Version, it is interesting that most other translations and Hebrew interpretations of the act renders it as "to be his wife" (*isha* meaning both "wife" and "woman") (see La Bible, Française Courante, New International Version, Revised Standard Version and Authorized Version).

There is a definite transition in the status of Hagar after she has been given to Abraham. It seems clear that it is the sexual act between Hagar and Abraham which changed her status from a handmaid to something else. Why did the Hebrew not render this as *pilegesh*? In those polygamous societies in which older wives participate in the marriages of their junior cowives, Hagar here would be considered a wife, because Sarah gave her to Abraham to have sex with him. Yet one may argue quite rightly that Hagar in Hebrew society did not become a wife, since she was not eligible. Hagar was a foreigner and a slave. None of the marriage requirements was performed. The practice of slaves sleeping with their masters was quite common, but apparently there was a distinction between wives and concubines. While biblical scholars recognize this distinction, I will demonstrate below that translators from polygamous societies will interpret this passage according to the way in which local polygamy is understood. Few translations render this passage as concubine. However, if Hebrew and other translations are to be followed and Hagar is translated as wife here, why not translate all other references of concubines as wives with such qualification as is contextually required—so the argument goes on! But let us return to Hagar for a while!

On becoming pregnant, Hagar, a mere slave, changes her status to concubine or wife, depending on the value system of the reader. The Bible reports that Hagar became haughty and nasty to Sarah:

> Abraham had intercourse with Hagar and she became pregnant. When she found out that she was pregnant, she became proud and despised Sarah. (Gen. 16:4–5)

No detail is given as to how Hagar despised Sarah. How should we interpret the relationship between the two? For some to whom polygamy is an acceptable form of marriage, Hagar is but a second or junior wife of Abraham, who, when things are going well for her, boasts to her cowife. Nothing strange. Sarah, on the other hand, is the senior jealous wife who exploits Hagar when it suits her and then dumps her when the problem is solved. For others, Sarah is the kind of woman that Margaret Atwood portrays in her novel, *The Handmaid's Tale.* She is conditioned by society to believe that her worth is dependent on her ability to produce children. In Atwood's words, she and other women such as Rachel and Leah are conditioned by society to think of themselves as "containers, it is only the insides of our bodies that are important." With such thinking, Sarah sees Hagar as an instrument for meeting her own needs—in today's idiom, one may say a disposable instrument. It is an issue of women struggling against each other in order to fulfill what society has designed for them.

PATRIARCHY

The study of Old Testament women in Hebrew polygamous society is tainted with patriarchal bias. One significant area of bias is the fact that we know very little about the women in the Old Testament polygamous systems. Very often we are just given names of the men and told that the man had so many wives and concubines. In this study I have failed to define what a concubine was; an attempt to study Sarah and Hagar in order to understand the difference between their marital status was of little use. What that suggests to me is that, without reconstructing the society in which these women lived, we gain no new knowledge about the Old Testament system of polygamy. Mavumilusa Makanzu, in his book *Can the Church Accept Polygamy?*, makes the following statement:

> When we talk about polygamy, we are simply talking about women. We can never understand why our ancestors were polygamous till we thoroughly grasp the status of women in traditional society. This is because marriage, in all its diverse forms, is always closely linked to the status assigned to women by society and to the place they were occupying in the minds and hearts of men. (9)

Some scholars have the opinion that women in the Old Testament marriage system were mainly valued for their sexuality and fertility (Bird). Polygamy, therefore, ensured a constant source of procreative gratification to the men, including compensation for those periods when some of the women had to observe life-cycle rituals of sexual abstinence such as menstruation and childbirth. Polygamy also guaranteed that the men would have descendants in their names. It is said that the first commandment, "Be fruitful and multiply" (Gen. 1:28), is addressed to men and not to women.

POLYGAMY AT LOGGERHEADS: BIBLE TRANSLATION

Bible translators are seriously limited by our ignorance of the distinction between wives and concubines in the context of the Old Testament. I implied that the Old Testament had established procedures for marrying wives, but soon I found out that there were many other means by which wives were obtained. In some cases, wives and concubines were both obtained by the same means, such as war captives. Two major problems face the translator. On one hand, the concept of concubinage is completely foreign to some polygamous societies, and on the other hand, the Bible does not give enough information to enable the Bible translator to interpret the word "concubine." To add to the difficulty, the other translations in major languages such as English and French are inconsistent in their translations of "wife" or "concubine," as shown in the case of Hagar above. The definition of the word "concubine" in Bible dictionaries and concordances is vague. As a result, there are several divergent translations of this term, not only in the Western languages, but even more so in African languages and cultures.

Sixteen East African translators were asked to review and translate the word *pilegesh* as found in "He had seven hundred wives, princesses and three hundred concubines" (1 Kings 11:3). The results can be summarized as follows. Three Kenyan languages, Gikuyu, Ragoli, and Luyia used a borrowed word from Swahili, *suria*. Indeed, the word *suria* means "concubine" in Swahili, but the practice of concubinage is virtually unknown to the traditional lives of these cultures. When asked for its meaning, those people unfamiliar with the usage of the word in Swahili did not know it. Kimeru (Kenya) used a generic word for woman. Chigogo in Tanzania also used the generic word for woman.

Luganda (Uganda) used the term for house servant. Karamajong, Teso, and Masaba, all neighboring Ugandan languages, preferred the terms used for widow inherited in a levirate marriage. Rutoro (Uganda) and Pokoot (Kenya) used the term for a second wife. Turkana (Kenya) and Lunyore (Kenya) both used the terms for a wife for whom dowry is still to be paid. Ruhaya (Tanzania) used the terms for secret lover—no dowry is required and the relationship is illicit. The Kuria (Kenya-Tanzania) used a term for a sex tutor—basically a partner of the opposite sex whom the culture permits practically to initiate a young person who is preparing for marriage. These results reflect considerable variation on the translation of *pilegesh*.

It is not unusual that the exact equivalents for translating certain biblical concepts into receptor languages are missing. However, what we see above is different and perhaps a more serious problem than the mere lack of exact equivalents. There is considerable variation among African groups in their lifestyles and in the nature of their social institutions. In fact, many are pluralistic and combine more than one system. Additionally, African societies are not static. In fact, they are changing much too rapidly. Even in the area of polygamy, there are many variations. With this in mind, it is significant to find that the Hebrew idea of concubinage is still strange to most East Africans. However, the society translates the Hebrew marriage system through the eyes of their own culture. African translators that I worked with often did not even bother to explore what the equivalent in Hebrew culture could have been, or to isolate the cases in which there were similarities and differences.

In his study of the Bangwa of Cameroon, Brain (114) reports that "all women are married in Bangwa. Here we have no widows, no spinsters, no concubines. A baby girl is betrothed at birth. A man dies and his widow is automatically the wife of the heir. Even an old woman is technically somebody's wife."

The translators quoted above were reported to share this Bangwa concept, with a number of local modifications. Among the Abaluyia of western Kenya, there was no concept of concubinage or prostitution in traditional society. The words used for both are borrowed from Swahili. The term for prostitution, *malaya*, is now widely known. However, concubinage is still not known in East Africa, because the society regards any women in a polygamous marriage as a wife. Among the Luo, a woman married within the clan is referred to as the wife of every man in that clan. In Maragoli traditional life, an infertile man had his brother secretly father children for him. The brother would make various visits to the man's compound, while the infertile man would pretend that nothing was happening.

The Abakuria (Kenya/Tanzania) translated "concubine" with a local term, *ebiroro*. They explained that in their culture, sex is permitted between young circumcised adults. A young circumcised man may be introduced to sex by an older circumcised married woman. Likewise a young circumcised woman is initiated by an older circumcised married man. This practice ensures that young people do not enter into marriage sexually ignorant. It also completes the circumcision ritual.

The Abakuria translated the word *pilegesh* according to their own belief system. They focused on the non-permanence of the *ebiroro* relationship. They understood the word "concubine" to mean a non-permanent sexual relationship and interjected their own practice of *ebiroro* into the translation of the Hebrew *pilegesh*. That may be because they did not understand the Hebrew meaning or did not distinguish the Hebrew practice of polygamy from their own.

CONCLUSION

The dilemma of Bible translation and interpretation hinges on whether to mold a text to conform to one's cultural value system, or whether to translate a passage literally at the expense of not being understood or creating confusion. As I have illustrated in this study of Old Testament polygamy, the meaning of the text is dependent upon the values of the person reading it and the applications to which it is put. In other words, translators influence the text. Bible translation thus far is still a preserve of men. Apart from a handful of female missionaries in third-world countries, most major translations are done by men. Thus, unless women also get into the area of Bible translation, the thought system of women will remain unreflected in the text which we receive. The language of the Bible will also remain masculine until the women take up the will to rise and influence this aspect of the Christian's base. I wonder how *pilegesh* would be translated if there were women, including those who feel like Hagar, among the translators!

REFERENCES

Achtemeier, Paul J., ed. *Harper's Bible Dictionary*. San Francisco: Harper and Row, 1985.

Atwood, Margaret. *The Handmaid's Tale*. Boston: Houghton Mifflin Company, 1986.

Bird, Phyllis A. "Images of Women in the Old Testament." In *The Bible and Liberation*, edited by Norman K. Gottwald. Maryknoll, New York: Orbis Books, 1984.

Brain, Robert. *Bangwa Kinship and Marriage*. Cambridge: Cambridge University Press, 1972.

Gottwald, Norman K., ed. *The Bible and Liberation*. Maryknoll, New York: Orbis Books, 1984.

Hillman, Eugene. *Polygamy Reconsidered: African Plural Marriage and the Christian Churches*. Maryknoll, New York: Orbis Books, 1975.

Kanyoro, Rachel M. "Women and Religion." Report No. 10, Kenya NGO, World Conference of the UN, Decade for Women. Nairobi, 1985.

Lutahoire, Sebastian N. *The Human Life Cycle among the Bantu*. Makumira Publication, 1974.

Mackenzie, John S. *Dictionary of the Bible*. New York: Macmillan Publishing Company, 1965.

Makanzu, Mavumilusa. *Can the Church Accept Polygamy?* Accra: Asempa Publishers, 1983.

Meyers, Carol L. "The Roots of Restriction: Women in Early Israel." In Gottwald, *The Bible and Liberation*.

Onaiyekan, John. "Marriage Customs in the Old Testament." In Amewowo, ed. *Biblical-Pastoral Bulletin*. WCFBA. Togo: Lomé, 1981.

Pobee, John S., and Barbel von Wartenberg-Potter. *New Eyes for Reading: Biblical and Theological Reflections by Women from the Third World*. Oak Park, Illinois: Meyer Stone Books; Geneva: World Council of Churches, 1986.

Robison, David, ed. *Good News Concordance*. Swindon: British and Foreign Bible Societies, 1983.

Tamez, Elsa. "The Woman Who Complicated the History of Salvation." In Pobee and Potter, *New Eyes for Reading*.

Tienou, Tite. *The Theological Task of the Church in Africa*. Achimota, Ghana: African Christian Press.

Young, Robert, ed., *Young's Analytical Concordance*. United Societies for Christian Literature. London: Lutterworth Press, 1975.

Wagner, Gunter. *The Bantu of Western Kenya*. London: Oxford University Press, 1970.

7

Polygamy: A Feminist Critique

Anne Nasimiyu-Wasike

Polygamy is a sensitive issue in Africa, and it has been debated by different disciplines of human sciences. Some scholars are very sympathetic and would like to see the Christian church accept polygamy as another form of valid marriage and the members within this institution baptized if they so desire. For example, the Anglican church, inspired by pastoral concern for the people in polygamous households, has had to reverse its stand of 1888. In 1988, the Lambeth Conference reversed its decision of withholding baptism from polygamous households. Now this possibility is open to them, but under the conditions inspired by the monogamous ideal.[1] It has to be realized that the importance here is placed on the pastoral rather than on the doctrinal understanding of marriage.

On the other hand, orthodox scholars have accepted the monogamous form of marriage as the only valid and recognizable Christian marriage without allowing for any exceptions. This is the Roman church's stand on the issue of polygamy and baptism.

The term "polygamy" is employed in this reflection in its popular usage, that is, as the marriage of one man and several women simultaneously, although anthropologists would define such a marriage "polygyny." This reflection is divided into two main parts. The first part will focus on some of the traditional purposes or aims of polygamy in Africa as given by various scholars.[2] Each purpose or aim will be followed by my critique of it. The aims include the recapturing and expanding of lost immortality, the search for male progeny, the desire to accumulate wealth, the strict division of labor, the religious duty to ancestors, and the enhancing of women's dignity. The second part will investigate the biblical view on polygamy by looking briefly at the polygamous stories found in the Scriptures to see whether or not these stories support the institution of polygamy. Secondly, the study will examine African women's views on polygamy, and finally, it will give a feminist theological critique of polygamy.

In patriarchal traditional Africa, it was every man's ideal to increase the number of his wives and thus recapture and expand his immortality. It was believed that those who die are reborn in their children. Therefore, it was important to have children in order to perpetuate this line. Many wives and many children meant stronger "immortality" for that family. It was assumed that the man with many descendants had the strongest possible manifestation of immortality, as his personal immortality was kept in the physical world by his numerous descendants long after he was dead.[3]

As a result of having many wives and many children, males enjoyed privileged and respectable positions in society. In the patriarchal system, women were valued only in relation to men. A woman's procreative power was important not for her own sake, but for strengthening the husband's power or immortality and for giving him a privileged and prestigious status in society. The woman was looked upon as the vessel of life or a fertile field in which a man planted his seeds. The more children she bore, the better for the man; the more wives (fields) the man had, the more children he was likely to beget. This concept of woman as a field of production led to the requirement of virginity on the woman's wedding day,[4] and the payment of bridewealth for the woman by the family of the husband-to-be. Virginity was at least an insurance that the field was whole and intact and should therefore give maximum yield.

Children were seen as the glory of marriage, but that glory

was first and foremost the glory of man. The barren woman was considered a dead-end and useless to the community. In some communities she was scorned and at times labelled a witch. In other communities she was looked at with pity and given children whom she could raise as her own, or she was encouraged to pay a dowry for a young woman who could in turn bear children for her. Whatever other qualities, gifts, and talents a woman might possess, the inability to procreate reduced her to the status of a non-person. If a man was unable to bear children, however, his case was not as tragic as that of a barren woman. One would only hear discrete whispers about it, and the man's brother could go secretly into the wife and children would be born for him.

A childless marriage was considered meaningless, and the man was pressured into polygamy. He would either return the barren wife to her parents and demand the refund of the bride-wealth in order to marry a second wife (successive polygamy), or, if he was wealthy, he simply married a second wife as well (simultaneous polygamy).

How would they know it was a male problem?

In most patriarchal African communities, children belonged to the man. For example, among the Babukusu, if a marital union failed, the wife would return or be returned to her family of origin, and if subsequently she had children, her former husband would pay her family three heads of cattle for a baby girl and two heads of cattle for a baby boy. This shows a woman to be a field which is loaned out by her family to the family of her husband. In this example and in many other African communities, it was the husband's lineage and the women's family who benefitted from the woman's procreative ability. The woman was a valuable commodity owned first by the male members of her family and, later, by her husband and his family.

Traditionally, during the process of socialization and internalization of community values, children were indoctrinated into talking, acting, feeling, valuing, and relating in ways that suited their respective sex roles as dictated by society. Boys were to emulate their fathers, while girls were to follow carefully in the footsteps of their mothers. There were taboos to ensure that everything was carried out according to the society's regulations. These taboos still have a strong influence on African people today. African women still see themselves as lacking identity when they are without children or unmarried.

The feminist interpretation of polygamy differs from a man's interpretation. The system exploits women for the benefit of men. The more subordinates and dependents the man had, the prouder he was, and the higher and mightier his personality soared. Therefore, it was good for a man to add to the number of his women whenever it suited him, or whenever his economic means would allow. Such an attitude was accepted as a respectable social norm by both women and men. This led to a polygamous man enjoying a prestigious and privileged social position. The women are servers and maintainers of the system that continues to relegate them to inferior status in society.

In conclusion, the expanding and strengthening of immortality through polygamy was and is primarily, if not exclusively, a male ideal, as the beneficiaries of that institution were and are primarily, if not exclusively, males. Women wanted to bear many children in order to serve and please the masters and husbands. Such an interpretation is also borne out by research carried out in selected countries of black Africa among high school and college students as to how many children they would like to beget.[5] The highest percentage of male students wanted to beget as many children as their procreative capacity would allow, whereas the highest percentages of female students wanted to have a limited number of children, that is, between three and six.

Secondly, the search for male progeny encouraged men to add to their number of wives. In patriarchal societies, male children were and are much more valued than female children. Inheritance was solely a male prerogative. Female children had and have no significance in genealogies. The father was and is believed to live on only in his male children as he was remembered from one generation to the next. A woman, therefore, who bore only female children was held in low esteem. The whole blame for failing to bear sons was levelled against her head, she was considered a failure by her society, and shame and guilt were heaped on her. The community advised the man to marry another wife or more wives in search for male children. Girls were considered as children who could not build their parents' homes.[6] In marriage, girls became wives to their husbands' clans, while their ties with their fathers' clans gradually disappeared.

Despite the scientific discoveries which have proved that the male chromosomes are responsible for determining a child's sex, some African men still blame women for a child of the unwanted sex.[7] Although female children are needed as mothers and wives to society, they are only of secondary value. The belief that women are the ones who determine the child's sex will change only gradually, if at all, due to long-held philosophical presuppositions which are embodied in the cultural themes of the people.

Thirdly, polygamy was encouraged in the society by the desire of men to accumulate wealth. In both agrarian and pastoral cultures, in which production depended on the number of hands, it was necessary to have several wives and many children to share the workload. In most cases, it was the rich families which were made up of polygamous marriages. Many wives and children were needed to till the land and tend the cattle. The size of the land under cultivation, as well as the number of heads of cattle, sheep, and goats, depended, to a large extent, on the number of wives and children a man had. Modern technology has improved methods of cultivation, and in most cases workers are employed to do the work on the farm. The nomadic pastoralists are also beginning to settle into schemes by which to implement the new technologies.

This idea of increasing the number of wives in order not to overburden the first wife with work and to increase crop production only enhances the concept of inequality and subordination of women to men. There is no partnership in this relationship, and women are like slaves working to enrich their husbands and masters.

Fourthly, sex-oriented division of labor was another factor which justified the practice of polygamy in the traditional Africa. Traditionally, work was sex-oriented. Men did the heavy and physically demanding jobs such as clearing land for cultivation, felling trees, going to war, protecting the homesteads against enemies, and hunting wild animals. Women did the cultivation, the planting, weeding, harvesting, and domestic chores. Women are physically and biologically different from men, but this does not make them inferior to men, as has traditionally been assumed.

This sex-oriented division of labor was so strict in African communities that taboos were created to maintain and protect the status quo. For example, it was a taboo for African men to cook in their homes. Therefore, a man with only one wife would have nobody to cook for him when his wife visited her family and other relatives, or when she was sick and unable to fetch water from the river, cut firewood, and cook.

The strict division of labor according to sex led to the stereotyping of women as loyal, docile, dependable, servers, child-bearers, and submissive housewives. Education and acculturation to Western ways of life are gradually influencing the African people. At present, some men are employed in jobs which were strictly women's jobs. For example, today African men are employed by hotels and restaurants as cooks, cleaners, and housekeepers. It is unfortunate that these very men still adhere to the taboos where their wives are concerned. They are reluctant to assist their wives in their own homes.

The fifth purpose for traditional polygamy was as a religious duty to the ancestors, an aim peculiar to the Tonga people.[8] A man was obliged to have two houses and a wife in each of them. One was under the protection of the spirits of the man's paternal grandmother's lineage, and the other was under the patronage of the spirits of the man's maternal lineage. It was essential and important that sacrifices and prayers be offered to those spirits in their respective houses. This reason for the justification for polygamy has long disappeared and does not have any hold on African people today.

The sixth reason for the practice of polygamy in traditional Africa emerged from the belief that women's worth and dignity were grounded in their marriage and procreative capacity. Unmarried or childless women were considered incomplete. It was also necessary for a woman to be under the protection and guidance of a man, first as a daughter, then as a first, second, or third wife. It was assumed that this was the only way in which a woman could find meaning, happiness, and fulfillment in life. In some communities, women outnumbered men, and this necessitated polygamy. A woman was considered weak, vulnerable, and defenseless, and thus needed a man for security, survival, and guidance. This reason for polygamy arises from the stereotyping of women and the belief that women are only fulfilled when under the dominion of men.

Finally, some scholars have suggested that polygamy protected African women and men against prostitution and reduced unfaithfulness.[9] Indeed, polygamy may prevent men from unfaithfulness and prostitution, but it does not do so with regard to women. A husband will be inclined to spend more time with his favorite wife, neglecting the other wives for weeks or months. It is not surprising that these women married to polygamous men had secret lovers.

Polygamy is still practiced throughout Africa, but the economic factors upon which traditional polygamy was based are changing very fast. The economy is moving from small-scale agriculture to large-scale machine-operated farms and from nomadic pastoral to irrigated settlement schemes. Africa is gradually becoming urbanized and industrialized, making it difficult for a poor man to afford the bride-wealth for even one wife. The rich men are the ones who still practice polygamy.

All the reasons advanced to justify polygamy in traditional Africa reveal a distorted relationship that has crippled both women and men in different ways and with different consequences.[10] The promotion and encouragement of polygamy were based on grounds that favored men by boosting their personality and reducing that of women to subservient and inferior status. The whole system supported and enhanced men's power and domination over women. Much of what has been written on the subject of polygamy has come from the male perspective and has emphasized the socioeconomic dimensions of the institution of polygamy while neglecting its religious dimension. In order to have a balanced view on this issue, both female and male perspectives must be sought and be included in the interpretation. The question of how polygamy fits in with the will of God for humankind must be tackled. The religious dimension of the issue of polygamy must include a dimension of God's will concerning this issue as expressed in African religious tradition and in the Bible.

From the creation myths found all over Africa, the evidence points to the reality that in the beginning God sanctioned a partnership relationship between man and woman.[11] Nowhere do we find God creating one man and giving him several wives. In most of the myths, God created man first and then woman. In some myths, the woman was created first and then the man. For example, among the Babukusu God created Mwambu first, then God saw that Mwambu was lonely and needed someone to talk to. Therefore, God created Selah to be Mwambu's partner.[12] Monogamy, from the African religious tradition, is God's will for humanity, because this was at the beginning of human life as expressed in the African creation myths.

BIBLE AND POLYGAMY

Monogamy emerges in the Old Testament as God's initial and final will for humanity. This message is powerful and clear in the creation story (Gen. 2:18). The Genesis creation story is reechoed in the African myths of the origin of human life. Several African myths on human creation affirm that God created one woman and one man to begin the generation of human life on earth. What is common in all these myths is that humanity was founded on equality and partnership between one man and one woman.

There are two creation stories in the Old Testament. In the first creation story, God called humanity into existence, male and female as the crown of all creation (Gen. 1:27). Women and men are equal partners created in the image and likeness of God. In the second creation story (Gen. 2:22), God created Eve from the rib of Adam and placed her at his side as a companion. The creation of Eve out of Adam's rib means that both Adam and Eve are made out of the same material. On seeing Eve, Adam exclaimed that at last he had a companion who was "flesh of his flesh and bone of his bones" (Gen. 2:23). Woman and man were created as a unity of the two in their common humanity, as is stated in Genesis 2:24: "Therefore, a man leaves his father and his mother and cleaves to his wife, and they become one flesh."[13] Woman and man are called to live in a communion of love, equality, reciprocity, and mutuality.

From these creation stories of the Jewish people and the African people, monogamy emerges clearly as the ideal form of marriage for humanity and the only one that is sanctioned by God. Monogamy, therefore, is not a cultural product, but a foundational relational aspect that was meant to promote mutual dependence, complementary relationships, and mutual cooperation between woman and man.

Several scholars have seriously investigated the question of polygamy in the Bible. All of them agree that there is no explicit commandment on polygamy or monogamy in the Scriptures. Some have argued that an implicit form of rejection of polygamy runs through the Scriptures.[14] Other scholars have observed that in many cases the chosen people assimilated customs and institutions of the surrounding neighbors, although their call by God continued to guide them in their new awareness.[15] Polygamy may have been one of these institutions that were adapted by the Jewish people.

In many cases where polygamy is reported in the Old Testament, it is in a form of apology and criticism rather than exaltation. The authors of the Scriptures express a sense of regret and embarrassment as they narrate those events. Here, we shall just cite a few examples to illustrate this statement.

The author of Genesis reports Abraham's polygamy in a critical way. It was a poor human solution to Sarah's barrenness, was not blessed, and portrayed lack of faith on the part of Sarah and Abraham. It led to estrangement between Sarah and Abraham and contempt, jealousy, and quarrelling between Sarah and Hagar (Gen. 16 and 21). This story clearly illustrates the evils of polygamy, and it implicitly rejects polygamy, because polygamy disrupts and creates unhappiness in the family.

Jacob's polygamy is no better. It generates bitter lives and unhappiness and creates rivalry and hatred in Jacob's home (Gen. 29:30–31). Although Leah and Rachel, Jacob's wives, were blood sisters, this did not prevent the squabble between them. Jacob spent more time with Rachel than with Leah; this preference of Rachel over Leah evoked much envy and quarrelling between the two wives. Jealousy and envy continued in the children, as Jacob favored Rachel's child Joseph over Leah's children (Gen. 37). Leah's children hated Joseph so much that they plotted to kill him, but finally they sold him into slavery.

The stories of polygamy in the books of Judges and Kings are narrated with gruesome realism. For example, in Judges 9:5 Abimelech wages a war of succession against his brothers. His maternal uncles assist him in murdering his sixty-nine brothers in order to establish his rule.

The stories of David's and Solomon's polygamy are stories which reflect apologies on the part of the authors. The Jewish kingdom is ruined because of David's and Solomon's polygamous involvements. David's sons killed each other over the question of inheritance (2 Sam. 14). Solomon's heart was led astray by his wives, and he followed their gods instead of Yahweh, the God of his ancestors (Kings 11:1–4). As a result, the kingdom was finally split into two. These are just a few examples to point out the negative light in which the polygamous stories appear in the Old Testament.

With resolute absoluteness the Old Testament gives serious warning messages against polygamy. It vividly points up the gruesome, gloomy images of polygamy and from one story of polygamy to another brings out the consequences of polygamous family life—for example, rivalries, jealousies, envies, favoritism, quarrels over inheritance, succession feuds, injustices, hatred, and murders. These realities are the experiences of African polygamous families as well. We shall talk more about this later.

By the time of the New Testament period, monogamy was probably the common form of marriage, although there may have been some simultaneous polygamous marriages. There are no explicit documents on simultaneous polygamy in the New Testament. It seems as if simultaneous polygamy was no longer a burning issue in the lives of the chosen people of the New Testament period. Successive polygamy was practiced, and the Jewish laws encouraged it. When Jesus was asked to respond to the issue of successive polygamy, he rejected it and criticized the Jewish law that was based on a patriarchal and polygamous understanding of marriage rather than on God's original plan for humanity.[16] The Jewish law that Jesus rejected took women's inferior status for granted. Jesus quotes the Genesis creation story to affirm his teaching on the equality, mutuality, and partnership of wife and husband.

In both the Old and New Testament, we do not find any documents in favor of either successive or simultaneous polygamy. In the Old Testament, the stories of polygamy are told as a warning to the Israelites about the evils and corruption arising from this institution. Again and again we see polygamy being rejected and monogamy emerging as the original plan of God for humanity. The Scriptures are written from the patriarchal viewpoint and women as such are silent. African women's views on polygamy can be found in African wisdom, especially in the Proverbs. We shall now reflect on the African women's experience of polygamy.

POLYGAMY AND AFRICAN WOMEN

African men and their Western European and American male sympathizers have told their version of polygamy, but the women's view is rarely voiced. African women's views on polygamy differ from men's apologia for it and resonates with the view proposed by the Scriptures.

It has been taken for granted that African men speak for African women. Whatever men think and say to be good and right, women are supposed to affirm and support. Men are self-appointed spokespersons for women and children in every patriarchal society. It has always been stated that traditional African women accepted polygamy and encouraged their husbands to take a second or third wife. In fact, the taboos created by society with regard to husband-wife relationships are the ones that encouraged and forced women to ask for polygamy. Society educated women to believe that they were subservient to men, and that their purpose was to make men wealthy by bearing many children and producing great amounts of food. When a woman found herself unable to cultivate, plant, weed, and harvest enough food due to physical weakness and not having enough children to help her, she was forced to request her husband to bring another or more subordinates. In most cases, the first wife chose women whom she believed would not be rivals but would instead be subservient to her.

There has been a fatal resignation of women to their status in society. Some of them wished they were men instead of women. To confirm this notion, the following question was put to young and old, male and female Nigerians in a socioreligious survey: "If you could be born again, would you choose to be a man or a woman?"[17] The answers to this question were revealing. Forty-eight percent of the girls wanted to be born as boys, whereas only 6 percent of the boys wanted to be born as girls. On the other hand, only 57 percent of the women wanted to be born as women.[18] This shows that many women are not happy with their lot, despite their seeming acceptance of what society expects of them. They quietly reject and resent what society and men have imposed on them. This quiet disapproval was, however, always interpreted as an acceptance.

African women's rejection of polygamy was projected to their cowives. African proverbs reveal this reality. For example, among the Logbara people of Uganda, we find proverbs which state, "The tongue of cowives is bitter," "The tongue of cowives is pointed," or, "A cowife is the owner of jealousy!"[19] These proverbs are traditional wisdom based on women's experience in a polygamous setting. They bring out the sad reality that exists in the polygamous family. The feuds that issue forth are the results of women rejecting the institution of polygamy. Women are vulnerable and powerless in patriarchal societies. They are unable to attack the power of customs, traditions, and men that subjugate them to men and keep them in inferior and subordinate positions. The cowife becomes the object of the woman's projected hatred for the system of polygamy, and this causes squabbling among women. This reality, like that of the Old Testament stories of polygamy, leads to bitter fights, endless intrigues, and constant fear of being poisoned or killed by witchcraft or magical powers. These fears have been reflected in several works by African authors. For example, the woman in Okot p'Bitek's poem says:

> The woman I share my husband with . . .
> I won't deny

I am a bit jealous
Lying is no good
We all suffer
From a touch of jealousy.
Jealousy seizes us
And makes us feverish.[20]

Another woman from Senegal lamented when she was having a miscarriage thus:

I am not ill: I am only the victim of witchcraft meant for my death. My husband's co-wives and lovers are to blame for it. . . . They have made some plots against me, so that he would leave me. And a proof of this lies in the fact that my husband has had no sex with me since when I was in my first month of pregnancy.[21]

This example illustrates the truth about polygamous families. It is a world of uncertainties, jealousies, and rivalries. There problems are passed on from women to their children, who continue the squabbling among themselves. The peace, harmony, and unity in this respect belongs to a Utopian world.[22]

The squabbles and fights of women against women keep them disunited, powerless, weak, and suspicious of each other. It is only by uniting and focusing on the common enemy that women will be able to expose the evils of polygamy.

On the other hand, there are some young educated women who are choosing polygamy. This relationship does not accord with the traditional understanding of polygamy. It is, rather, an arrangement between the young woman and the man of her choice. She can have a number of men as she pleases and can drop them if she does not like them. Although the young woman is rejecting the African woman's traditional roles, she, in turn, is ending up in new forms of enslavement and exploitation. The economic and social changes and pressures are the contributing factors to this new form of polygamy.

When Christianity came to Africa, it taught that monogamous marriage was the only valid and recognizable marriage. Polygamous men who sought baptism were advised to choose one of the women for a wife and send the others away as non-wives.[23] To dismiss the African women in polygamous unions as non-wives is to fail to recognize the concept of marriage in the African traditional beliefs. In African reality, it is not very easy for a woman who has been married once to find a single man to marry her, especially if she has had children in her first marriage. The women in polygamous marriages were the most disadvantaged individuals. It is unjust and inhuman for a mother of ten or two who has been with her husband, the only one she knows, for several years, and who has been duly married according to customary law, to be cast aside as a non-wife because the husband desires baptism.

The church's concern all along is for the polygamous man, but not for the women in the polygamous marriages. Since each of the wives is married only to one man, could they not be considered for baptism if they so desired? In the case of a polygamous man seeking baptism, all his wives could be consulted, and all of them together could make the decision. If the wives freely choose to separate from their husband, this should be encouraged, but for the women who do not favor separation, their wish should be respected, and baptism could be suspended until there is a common concession. In cases where polygamous men have sought baptism, the wives' decision was not sought, and some of these women became bitter at the church for separating them from their husbands. In conclusion, the teaching and practice of the church on marriage does not enhance the position of women, especially those who find themselves in a polygamous union.

A FEMINIST THEOLOGICAL CRITIQUE

Social and economic changes are reshaping the outward appearance of African society, but old religious and philosophical presuppositions persist in its collective subconscious. Therefore, it is important to raise the consciousness of the people by educating them and offering them alternatives so that they can gradually develop different values—values founded on the dignity of all, children, women, and men, and which are Christ-centered.

Today, in theological circles, there is an attempt to incorporate the Christian message into the African culture. The debate is centered on the question of inculturation, indigenization, or contextualization. Some of the proponents of African culture have invested high stakes in the issue of polygamy. They interpret and use polygamy "as the touchstone of genuine indigenization" or inculturation.[24] To use polygamy as a criterion for inculturation is to miss the whole point of inculturation. Before we delve into the issue of polygamy in relation to inculturation, it is better to give a working definition of inculturation.

Inculturation is a person's conversion to Jesus Christ within his or her own cultural context. This is the essential element present in the various definitions of inculturation currently proposed. A person is called to follow Christ within her or his own community in a radically new way. One sees how Christ gives meaning to her or his culture by purifying, sanctifying, elevating, and restoring it to wholeness. The beauty, richness, and goodness that already exist in the culture have been used in expressing the gospel message so that the people's life is renewed and the vitality of the whole church enhanced. This process of inculturation is similar to the incarnation of Christ, which is a prime model of contextualization.[25]

God's love for humanity was revealed in Jesus Christ. Jesus came to the world as human in flesh and blood in order to restore humanity and the whole of creation to new life and to the original plan of God. Through Jesus, an intimate relationship was established between God and humanity (Eph. 5). By Jesus' incarnation, women and men were freed from servitude to sin and death, and human life was fully divinized.[26]

In Christ, all peoples and their cultures are drawn into God. Christ challenges every culture today as he did the Jewish culture in his lifetime. He denounced whatever enslaved people and rejected anything that kept people from appreciating their basic human dignity. For us to be participants in the mission of God through Christ, we have to denounce the degrading and segregating systems created by people. These are systems within our cultures which legitimize the exploitation of some while preserving the privileged status, prestige, and power of others. Polygamy is one of those systems that legalize the inferiority and subordination of women to men. Christ's message is one that gives full life to all and mends the brokenness of our humanity. Polygamy reflects the brokenness of our humanity, and as such it cannot be accommodated by Christianity. The Christian message recognizes that women and men are equal sharers in humanity and that both are made in the image and likeness of God. It carries within it a radical vision of human mutuality, reciprocity, and cooperation. In principle, Christianity can make an important contribution to the emancipation of African women, particularly with regard to the issue of polygamy.[27]

It is essential that the advocates of polygamy give a critical analysis to the grounds of their defense. Most of the modern proponents of polygamy are men, who may alienate a whole community of women from the social and educational changes which lead towards a more just world.[28] The Christian message, on the contrary, rejects polygamy and calls for a fair and just treatment of both women and men.

In this reflection, we have seen that polygamy was practiced in both Jewish and African cultures. In all these cultures' creation myths, it was clear that the original will of God for humanity was equal partnership and mutual relationship between women and men. Polygamy came about as a human response to social, economic, religious, and personal needs and was based on distorted human relationships between women and men. Christ came to bind and heal human brokenness and to restore humanity to integrated wholeness. To inculturate the Christian message into African cultures is to be able to establish a creative process in which a new Christian culture gradually emerges. The task includes a careful discernment of the valid elements of the African people's way of life so as to incorporate them into the Christian message, and a rejection of those elements and institutions which rob some people of their freedom of thought and action and render them passive recipients of directives concerning what they are allowed to do, where, and under what circumstances.

NOTES

1. Anne Nasimiyu-Wasike, *A Report on ANA's Second Polygamy Consultation* (5 December, 1988), 34.

2. The various functions of polygamy surveyed here come from several authors; e.g., John Mbiti, *African Religions and Philosophy* (London: Heinemann, 1969) and *Love and Marriage in Africa* (Great Britain: Longman, 1973); David G. Maillu, *Our Kind of Polygamy* (Nairobi: Heinemann, 1988); and Bénézet Bujo, "Polygamy in Africa: A Pastoral Approach," *ANA Newsletter* 106, 1987.

3. John Mbiti, *African Religions and Philosophy*, 142.

4. Walter Trobisch, *My Wife Made Me a Polygamist*, 7th ed. (Germany: Kohl/Rhein, Editions Trobisch, 1980), 21.

5. "Contributions to the Rights and Wrongs of African Women," in *Pro-Mundi Vita Dossiers* (October 1979).

6. Dr. Better Ekeya, in an oral interview in 1987, informed me that among the Iteso there is a proverb which compares a baby girl to a frog that will soon leap away.

7. Pia Njoki's Case in *Daily Nation*, 1983.

8. Arthur Phillips, ed., *Survey of African Marriage and Family Life* (London: Oxford University Press, 1953), 59.

9. Mbiti, *Love and Marriage in Africa*, 143.

10. Elisabeth Moltmann-Wendel and Jürgen Moltmann, "Becoming Human in New Community," in *The Community of Women and Men in the Church*, ed. Constance E. Parvey (Philadelphia: Fortress Press, 1983), 34.

11. For example, the Ganda myth of Kintu and Nambi, the Agikuyu myth of Gikuyu and Mumbi, the Dinka myth of Garang and Abuk, and the Ababukusu myth of Mwanbu and Selah.

12. Daryll Forde, *African Worlds*, 8th Impression (International African Institute, Great Britain: Oxford University Press, 1976), 29.

13. Genesis 2:24 is the only verse on marriage that is quoted four times in the Bible: Matt. 19:4–5; Eph. 5:31; 1 Cor. 6:16; Mark 10:6–8.

14. Walter Trobisch, *My Wife Made Me a Polygamist*, 23.

15. William G. Blum, CSC, *The Unity of Christian Marriage Considered in Relation to the Polygamous Culture of Uganda* (Rome: Pontificia Universitas Lateranensis, 1973), 42.

16. Ibid., 422.

17. "To Be Or Not To Be a Woman—That Was the Question," in *Pro Mundi Vita Dossiers* (African Dossier No. 9, October 1979), 4.

18. Ibid., 4.

19. A. T. Dalfovo, *Lugbara Proverbs*, 58, 59.

20. Okot p'Bitek, *Song of Lawino* (Nairobi, Kenya: Afropress Ltd., 1966), 24.

21. R. Guena, Ch. de Preneuf and Reboul. Aspetti Psicopatologici della gravidanza aperto (Florence: Vallechi, 1974).

22. Some male scholars have presented African polygamy as a source of the great African virtues of solidarity, unity, harmony, and hospitality. Cf. Eugene Hillman, *Polygamy Reconsidered: African Plural Marriage and the Christian Churches* (Maryknoll, New York: Orbis Books, 1975).

23. Francisco Javier Urrutia, "Can Polygamy Be Compatible with Christianity?" *African Ecclesial Review* 23, No. 5 (1981): 277.

24. Lamin Sanneh, *West African Christianity: The Religious Impact* (Maryknoll, New York: Orbis Books, 1983), 248.

25. James O. Buswell III, "Contextualization: Theory, Tradition and Method," in *Theology and Mission*, David J. Hesselgrove, ed. (Grand Rapids, Michigan: Baker Books House, 1978), 92.

26. John Gorski, M.M., "Is World Mission Still Urgent Today?" *Omnis Terra* 22, No. 187 (April 1988): 200.

27. Lamin Sanneh, *West African Christianity*, 249.

28. Ibid., 249.

8

Social Changes and Women's Attitudes toward Marriage in East Africa

Judith Mbula Bahemuka

INTRODUCTION

Marriage provides for the formation of families, the basic social unit around which much of the social structure is organized, and which performs the essential functions of producing children and socializing them. Since marriage is the basis of the family, it is essential for social organization. Marriage fulfills important functions for the individual. It provides a socially recognized paired relationship that is relatively permanent, the stability of which is supported by many social institutions. It is within a successful marriage that the individual finds his or her material, sexual and psychological needs most effectively satisfied. Marriage also provides an oasis of satisfaction in an impersonal mass society that is characterized by a relative lack of primary relations and institutions (Saxton, 277).

In East African countries, marriage is still considered a cov-

Judith Mbula Bahemuka, a Kenyan, teaches in the Department of Sociology at the University of Nairobi. She has a doctorate in Sociology and has done extensive research into African traditional cultures.

enant between two individuals, between two families and even clans. It is a socially legitimate sexual union, publicly announced and undertaken with some idea of permanence. The marriage bond ties the two individuals together, spells out reciprocal rights and obligations between the spouses, and between spouses and their children. Mbiti argues that marriage is the focus of existence. In each marriage, all the members of the family meet: the departed, the living, and those who are yet to be born. In every marriage, the whole African family is deeply involved, and therefore, marriage to the African is a religious act. Through marriage, the African family, which from time immemorial was the cradle of religious beliefs and activities, was kept intact.

Traditional African marriage was also seen as the center of the society. It was not the sexual union that constituted marriage, but rather, as Mbiti writes:

> All the dimensions of time meet here, and the whole drama of history is repeated, renewed and revitalized . . . Therefore, marriage is a duty, a requirement from the corporate society, and a rhythm of life in which everyone must participate. Otherwise, he who does not participate in it is a curse to the community, he is a rebel and a lawbreaker, he is not only abnormal but "under-human." Failure to get married under normal circumstances means that the person concerned has rejected society and society rejects him in return. (133)

Every African marriage called for procreation. There was no marriage in the African sense unless the fruit of that marriage could be seen. It was the duty of every married couple to reproduce and to contribute to society by giving it new members. The parents were biologically reproduced in their children; they contributed to perpetuating the chain of humanity. Marriage and procreation were therefore seen as unity, a unity which attempted to recapture, even if partly, humanity's lost gift of immortality. This meant that through marriage and procreation, the African became immortal, as the name was perpetuated through generations. One can, therefore, argue that most African societies were eponymous. They supported, praised, and sanctioned marriage, and at times enforced it.

THE PROBLEM

East Africa, and indeed most of Africa south of the Sahara, has been caught in what has come to be known as "the wind of change." The change has been experienced in different spheres of the African's life—political, cultural, social, economic, and religious. These have been brought about by agents of change which flooded most of the continent by the turn of the nineteenth century.

This short essay is not intended to be on social change per se, nor is it a psychological treatise on African women and their attitudes, nor even a castigation of polygamy as a social institution, but a critical approach to what is happening in East Africa to the institution of marriage, the changes that are taking place, and how women react to these changes.

My essay proposes, to a limited extent, to look at Christianity and marriage and the types of oppressive structures that have been created as a result of change.

AFRICAN MARITAL UNIONS

Marriage, as was argued earlier, was to the African an institution which provided the continuity of society. The African, being at pains to perpetuate *his* lineage, *his* clan, came up with different ways to make sure that every marriage produced children. The most common marital unions were monogamy, polygyny (as opposed to polygamy which includes polyandry), ghost marriages, child and "woman-to-woman" marriages.

Monogamy was always widespread among Africans. This, however, should not be taken to mean that monogamy was the *desired* form of marital union. There were factors related to the issue of monogamy. One such factor was that not everybody was wealthy enough to afford bride-wealth for more than one wife.

Polygyny was a sign of social prestige and wealth. It was, and still is, only the rich people in East Africa who can afford to pay bride-wealth for more than one wife. Polygyny also showed that the man could afford to keep his many wives in harmony and effectively bring up their children.

Ghost marriages were seen as social intervention if a young man died before getting married. To avoid discontinuity of his name, the family and clan got together and married a wife in the name of the deceased. A close relative was chosen to act as a genitor.

Of ghost marriages, Mbiti writes:

> If a son dies before he has been married, the parents arrange for him to get married "in absentia," so that the dead man is not cut off from the chain of life. It may not matter very much about the biological link: it is the mystical link in the chain of life which is supreme and most important. (144)

Ghost marriages were purely a way of preserving the name of the dead man. The family took care of the girl, and the children born to her assumed the dead man's name.

Child marriages were traditionally arranged in cases where an elderly couple bore an only son in their old age. The boy's father chose a girl for his son, and then proposed to the girl's family. This was done to ensure that before the father died, his son would have children to remember him. The girl was given to one of the relatives to act as a genitor until the son was old enough. It is important to note that in child marriages the father of the boy could not act as the genitor, since this would be tantamount to incest.

Woman-to-woman marriages, or social marriage between two women, were traditionally practiced by some communities in East Africa (such as the Agikuyu, the Akamba, and the Nandi of Kenya). This type of marriage was purely for procreation purposes. The woman who married was herself a legally married woman who was either barren or had given birth only to daughters. After initial consultation between herself and her husband, the two chose a girl whom they wanted to incorporate into their family. The woman, in her husband's presence, or in the presence of one of the clan elders, *designated* or *mentioned* the name of the girl to be the wife of her son who was never born. The woman's husband then approached the family of the girl and proposed to them. If the proposal was accepted, the girl was taken home by the couple after paying one bride-wealth.

The duty of looking for a genitor fell entirely on the woman's husband. The genitor normally was the eldest nephew of the husband. If a nephew was not available, another close male relative was chosen to act as a genitor. There were instances, however, when the woman arranged with her husband and allowed him to be the genitor. Even in such cases, the children born of the union were socially his grandchildren, for they were born, not to his name, but to his son's name. In this type of union, the man was allowed to marry a second wife of his own choice.

Woman-to-woman marriages were traditionally an important social phenomenon among the Africans. It was through such unions that Africans showed explicitly that they were at pains to try to perpetuate the family's name, and that societal continuity was paramount. The woman who designated a girl to be her son's wife wanted to see the name of her son, who was born socially but never biologically, perpetuated.

The foregoing is a brief discussion of some of the marital unions found among the East African peoples. There have not been any exhaustive studies on polyandry in the three East African countries, although there are some matriarchal societies at the borders of Tanzania in which anthropologists argue that polyandry may have been practiced on a limited scale.

Marriage can also be looked upon as a complex of customs that regulate and enhance the relationship between a couple and provide for the creation of a family. It also specifies the appropriate way of establishing a relationship, and inherent to it are provisions for terminating this type of relationship (Leslie, 14).

MARRIAGE AND SOCIAL CHANGE

Social change in East Africa has been uneven and has affected individuals and communities differently. Mbiti, discussing social change in Africa, writes:

Paradoxically, the individual is involved in the change and yet alienated from it. So he becomes an alien both to traditional life and to the new life brought about by modern change ... Africans also receive part of that culture and reject the other part; and they kick away part of their traditional culture while retaining the other part. (219)

Social change has affected some aspects of marriage, such as bride-wealth, preparation for marriage, rituals related to marriage, the purpose of marriage, marital unions, and the termination of the marriage covenant. It was earlier mentioned that procreation, not companionship, was the main objective of marriage. Mutual attraction of the young couple was not the determining factor for marriage. The whole family-clan was involved in each union, and society did its best to maintain the institution for social stability. Polygyny, in its traditional sense, can only be discussed in the light of African beliefs, the economy, sociocultural-political structures, and the African understanding of self and one's relation to others and the environment.

POLYGYNY AS A FORM OF MARRIAGE

Studies done in East Africa show that polygyny in its traditional form is declining (Kabwegyere and Mbula, Mbula, 1977), while other scholars argue strongly for a reconsideration of polygyny as an institution (Hillman, Kanyandago, Shorter, Njenga).

Polygyny, as a marital union, was necessitated by the African mode of production, in which each family was a unit of both consumption and production. The need for labor, and the very structures in which the division of labor was clear-cut, made it a must for a man to look for that extra labor force. Marriage of many wives, who would produce many children, became socially acceptable.

Polygyny was also a sign of wealth, and therefore pegged to the socioeconomic status of the individual men who could support more than one wife. Polygyny was also of value to those husbands whose wives could not produce children.

In some communities, polygyny was encouraged by women.

Among the Agikuyu of Kenya, it is the first wife who chooses a junior wife for her husband. By so doing, her status is elevated to that of a senior wife, and the junior wife respects her as a cowife. Polygyny is an institution which provides women with a chance of getting married. In cases where the second or third wife is a woman who has had children out of wedlock or from a prior marriage, the system provides a father figure for children who otherwise would be without a social father to bring them up.

POLYGYNY AND CHRISTIANITY

The most important agent of social change as far as marriage is concerned in Africa is Christianity. With the coming of Christianity to East Africa, people's ideas on marriage began changing. Christian marriage is, by definition, monogamous and indissoluble. This, however, has not always been the case. A brief history will demonstrate the facts.

In the early period of the development of Hebrew religion, the God of Israel was a god neither of fertility nor of procreation. The relationship between God and people had no sexual imagery. In the New Testament, God operated in a conspicuously non-sexual manner through God's Son, Jesus Christ, the Word made flesh. God's son was conceived by a virgin by the power of the Holy Spirit. The metaphor of marriage between God and God's people is found in the prophets. Hosea pleaded with Israel to be faithful to the marriage covenant with her husband God. In Isaiah 37:22 Israel is called, for the first time, "the virgin of the Lord," and it was the covenant relationship that was to be blessed with a son. This marriage metaphor continued in the New Testament in which Christ became the Bridegroom (Matt. 9:15; Mark 2:19–20; Luke 5:34–35). Christ was the Bridegroom, and the faithful had to cleave to him (Mbula, 1977, 128).

One can see how, in Christianity, marriage comes to be viewed as a divine gift requiring those who receive it to establish a lasting union. The union is called the "unity of flesh" and forms the basis for the understanding of sexual life in Christianity.

The church grew up within a predominantly monogamous world. In the early centuries of Christianity, marriage was not an exalted state of life. It was not until the twelfth century C.E. that marriage was proclaimed as one of the seven sacraments of the church. Of the early Christian church, Leslie writes:

> Sexual intercourse even in marriage was considered to be a necessary evil rather than a source of pleasure. It was necessary for the purpose of producing children and the virgins were idealized by the Church. At the fourth Council of Carthage, in A.D. 308, it was declared that bride and groom abstain from intercourse on their wedding night out of respect for the benediction. Later the period was extended to three nights. The couple could avoid the obligation by paying a moderate fee to the Church. (175–176)

It is to be noted with interest, however, that some early Christian emperors, including Pepin, Barbarossa, and Charlemagne, were all polygamists. In the sixth century C.E. the first prohibition of polygyny was promulgated in the Code of Justinian (Caincross, 1). However, this was not taken seriously, for later, Pope Gregory II, in a decretal in the year 726, laid down that "When a man has a sick wife who cannot discharge the marital functions, he may take a second one, provided he looks after the first one" (28).

It was after this that the early Fathers of the church started to work towards monogamy. They argued that polygyny limited the sexual freedom of the woman. Thomas Aquinas went so far as to compare human beings to animals, and to show that monogamy is the rule in the animal world wherever the male needs to exercise continued care over the offspring, while polygyny exists only where the male exercises no such care. He further argued that friendship involves a certain equality, and that in polygyny the "liberal friendship" proper to marriage is replaced by a "servile friendship" in which both equality and intensity of love are lacking. Finally, Aquinas argued that experience shows that the presence of several wives in the home tends to produce discord (Hastings, 9).

The following became the church's resolutions on marriage: The first, monogamous marriage was always a valid marriage, even if contracted under customary law. Secondly, in accepting the "Pauline Privilege" the church recognized that a valid natural marriage could be dissolved on the occasion when one partner was being baptized and it became morally or physically impossible to continue to live together. Thirdly, the church finally rejected plural marriages, but allowed a man to be baptized who put aside all his wives but one; the additional wives of an unbaptized man could not be baptized. The man was left free to choose which one of his wives he was going to keep, so long as the one chosen was willing to be baptized; their marriage would only be valid if celebrated before a priest and two witnesses (Hastings, 9).

After the Reformation, things started taking a different shape. The Protestant churches, unlike the Roman Catholic church, for a long time had no clear-cut stand on polygyny. There were three major camps: those who stood for and supported polygyny as a form of marriage; those who totally rejected it; and those who held a more middle position. As late as 1534, the Anabaptists in Munster, Germany, proclaimed polygyny as divinely revealed and as the ideal form of marriage. The rest of the city stoned them to death, and the experiment was never repeated, for:

> it was greeted with unanimous revulsion and horror ... This condemnation (both then and subsequently) reflects a loathing for polygamy which is very deeply rooted in Western man. True, the idea of cohabiting both with a wife and one or more mistresses has often been tolerated and even covertly admired ... Polygamy has been strictly a taboo to Western man. (Caincross, 1)

On African soil, one of the most outspoken Protestant missionaries, Henry Venn, Secretary of the Church Missionary Society from 1841 to 1872, produced a memorandum on polygyny (1956) in which he said:

A state of polygamy is unlawful within the Church of Christ, even though commenced in ignorance.

1. Because it had been declared by God to be contrary to the Divine institution of marriage.

2. Because it has been pronounced adultery by Christ.

3. Because it is written: "Let every man have his own wife, and let every woman have her own husband." Therefore, a polygamist cannot be lawfully admitted by baptism into the Church of Christ. (Hastings, 12)

In 1910, at the World Missionary Conference (Edinburgh), the missionaries from Africa showed no tolerance at all for polygyny. They reported the following:

Our correspondents in Africa view with unanimous intolerance conditions of life which are not only unchristian, but are at variance with the *instinctive feelings of natural morality*. With them there can be no "question" of polygamy. It is simply one of the gross evils of heathen society which, *like habitual murder and slavery must at all costs be ended*. (Hastings, 15) (The italics are mine.)

There is no doubt that Christianity did not look favorably on polygyny. The other agent of social change which has influenced marriage in general is the economy.

POLYGYNY AND THE ECONOMY

One factor that limits mass polygyny is the institution of bridewealth. Not every eligible man can afford to marry several wives. It is also clear that with women being economically independent, it is not easy to convince a woman to marry a man who already has a wife.

Closely related to the economy is formal education for women. Studies have shown that most educated women opt for monogamous marriages.

POLYGYNY AND SOCIAL CLASS

Traditionally, polygyny provided new social status for the woman. In today's societies, social class is achieved and not prescribed. This means that polygyny can no longer be used as a status symbol. It is because of this that the practice of serial and sequential polygyny is becoming common. A man marries one wife legally, and lives with several mistresses at the same time. After a while, he divorces the wife and marries one of the mistresses. Although the mistresses may be treated better than the wife, they do not achieve the status of a wife. Sequential and serial polygyny is very common in urban areas of East Africa.

POLYGYNY, WOMEN, AND OPPRESSION

In this section, I would like to show that polygyny as an institution is oppressive to women, and that social structures support and uphold it to dominate women. Several concepts will be discussed to demonstrate that African polygyny is a thing of the past and should be discouraged. The concepts include:
— patriarchy
— religious beliefs
— functionalism
— production and reproduction
— decision making.

POLYGYNY AND PATRIARCHY

The concept of patriarchy was used by the sociologist Max Weber to describe a particular form of household organization in which the father dominated other members of an extended kinship network and controlled the economic production of the household (Barrett, 10). In patriarchal societies, descent is along the father's line, and therefore the man owns not only the means of production, but also his wife and her reproductive powers.

Several scholars have shown that patriarchy promotes the

male at the expense of the female. Firestone (20) argues that biological reproduction has its roots in the biological division of sexes, and that men dominate women. It is because of this domination that she emphasizes the need to revolutionize "reproduction technology" in order to free women from the burden of their biologically determined oppression (Barrett, 12).

Further, it has been shown that because of patriarchy, there is a tendency to stress male supremacy as male control over women's fertility, without a case being made as to why and how men acquired this control. In East Africa, patriarchy is at the root of polygyny. Young girls and boys are socialized to believe that boys are the preferred sex, that a woman will continue to produce children until she produces a boy, that the boy will eventually inherit his father's wealth, and the woman will become dependent on the son and her husband. The greater the number of boys, the better for the family.

Kuhn, in discussing patriarchy and women argues: "Many analyses to women's oppression designate the family as the crucial site of oppression and yet reduce it to an entity that is itself the product of the playing of forces where real operations lie elsewhere" (11).

If the African family is the site of oppression, it is important to look at other important variables that are at play and see whether patriarchy cannot be modified.

POLYGYNY AND RELIGIOUS BELIEFS

The African family is built on the strong pillars of the past, the present, and the future. The past is made up of our ancestors, those who have gone before us and yet are part of us! The present is central, as this is where procreation, marriage, and family are to be found. The future is in the loins of the youth, who will continue the family and the human community. Because of this belief, the present is seen as the continuation of the past and a prerequisite for the future. This trinitarian belief has a tremendous impact on women. Not knowing that it is the male who genetically determines the sex of the child, women frustrate themselves trying to produce an heir for their husbands.

It is notable that it is the husband's name and lineage that is perpetuated. Modern persons need not capture their lost immortality, and if they have to, it can be done not through oppressive structures like polygyny, but through spiritual strength and a firm belief in the person of Christ, who overcame death.

POLYGYNY AND FUNCTIONALISM

The sociologist Talcott Parsons has provided an analysis of the function of the family in society. He argues that:

> the family today has two main functions: to socialize children into society's normative system of values and to inculcate "appropriate" status expectations; to provide a stable emotional environment that will cushion the (male) worker from the psychological damage of the alienating occupational world. (Parsons and Bales, 11)

It is clear that within the family these functions are carried out by the wife and mother. It is also the woman who plays the effective "instrumental" role of earning the family's keep and maintaining discipline (Barrett, 189). Since the woman plays the expressive role, it is easy for her to combine this function with that of the "bread winner." In East Africa, one of the reasons for polygyny was to exploit the dual role of the woman as a mother and a laborer. This is becoming even more obvious today with many men migrating to towns and leaving women to act as household heads.

Production and reproduction in the household economy are not only important, but central to the understanding of women's oppression and polygyny. The two, however, should be seen in relation to decision-making patterns within African communities. Most major decisions affecting the family are made by men. One such decision is the number of children a couple should have. If a woman does not accept such a decision, the husband may decide to marry another wife. This, in itself, makes the woman vulnerable, and forces her to accept such a decision for the sake of family stability.

WOMEN'S ATTITUDES TOWARDS POLYGYNY

Women's attitudes towards polygyny are based on the individual woman's perception of the problem, her aspirations, and her expectations. At first glance at the problem, there is no doubt that women are their own worst enemies. They are enemies to themselves because:
— they help to perpetuate oppressive social structures;
— they socialize their children to understand that girls should be dependent and that boys should exercise supremacy;
— to save their families from hunger, they have to perform the dual role of mother and managers;
— they believe that it is of paramount importance to perpetuate the family name;
— they create an environment conducive to polygyny by involving themselves with already married men.

The attitudes, however, are not that easy to analyze. They are like a two-edged sword. On the one hand, women loathe polygyny; on the other hand, women are the perpetuators of the institution.

One of the strongest urges in human beings is the urge to love and to be loved. Women aspire to be loved and to love, to establish a family, bring up children, and live a happy life. At the same time, women expect the society to respect them, give them equal opportunities, and establish a community in which they can actualize their potential.

The attitudes, however, cannot be generalized. Individual perception of a problem is generally colored by the individual's social-philosophical awareness and psychological makeup. One can, therefore, conclude by arguing the following:

1. In East Africa, polygyny is not as prevalent as it had been previously, due to the changing attitudes of women.

2. Due to social change, sequential polygyny is on the

increase, and the custom of keeping concubines and mistresses is widely practiced in urban centers.

3. Women who are economically independent are less prone to become victims of polygyny.

4. The changing division of labor and modes of production are helping to reduce the incidence of polygyny.

5. Christianity, with its stress on monogamy, has done much to change people's attitudes towards polygyny. There is still a need to make Christianity more practical in Africa by making it a living message of the Good News and not simply "Dos and Don'ts."

Christ came to the world with a purpose, and he made this purpose clear:

> The Spirit of the Lord is upon me,
> because he has anointed me
> to preach the Good News to the poor.
> He has sent me to proclaim release to the
>   captives
> and recovering sight to the blind
> to set at liberty those who are oppressed.
>   (Luke 4:18; Isa. 61:1–2)

Finally, the singular important factor that can help minimize incidents of polygyny is the promotion of women's dignity. Women should be educated to appreciate their work, their God-given freedom, their talents, their vocation to bring Christ to Africa and conquer Africa for Christ.

REFERENCES

Bahemuka, Judith Mbula. *Our Religious Heritage.* London: Thomas Nelson and Sons Ltd., 1983.

Baker, Archibold G. *A Short History of Christianity.* Chicago: The University of Chicago Press, 1953.

Barrett, Michele. *Women's Oppression Today.* London: Redwood Burn Ltd., 1980.

Beechey, Veronica. "Some Notes on Female Wage Labor in Capitalist Mode of Production." In *Capital and Class* 3 (1977).

———. "On Patriarchy." In *Feminist Review* 3 (1979).

Bruegel, Irene. "What Keeps the Family Going?" *International Socialism* 2, no. 1 (1978).

Caincross, J. *After Polygamy Was Made A Sin.*

Hastings, Adrian. *Christian Marriage in Africa.* London: SPCK, 1973.

Kanyandago, Peter. *Documents of the African Episcopate on the Evangelization of African Customary Marriages. A Point of Departure for African Theology,* 1988.

Kirkpatrick, Clifford. *The Family as Process and Institution.* New York: Ronald Press Co., 1963.

Kuhn, Annette, and Ann Marie Wolpe, eds. *Feminism and Materialism.* London: Routledge and Kegan Paul, 1978.

Land, Hilary. "Who Cares for the Family?" *Journal of Social Policy* 7, no. 3 (1978).

Leslie, Gerald R. *The Family in Social Context.* New York: Oxford University Press, 1973.

Mbiti, John S. *African Religions and Philosophy.* London and Nairobi: Heinemann, 1969.

Mbula, Judith. "Penetration of Christianity into the African Family." M.A. thesis, Nairobi University, 1974.

————. "The Impact of Christianity on Family Structure and Stability: The Case of the Akamba of Eastern Kenya." Ph.D. thesis, Nairobi University, 1977.

Parsons, T., and Robert F. Bales. *Family Socialization and Interaction Process.* New York: The Free Press, 1956.

9

Sexuality and Women in African Culture

Lloyda Fanusie

INTRODUCTION

The age-old expression when one hears of the coming of a new baby—"It is a boy!" or "It is a girl!"—signifies joy that one more human being has joined the species. It is also a promise of the continuity of our race. Being aware of the divine will at work, our innate spiritual virtues encourage us to hope that this system will continue. We have hope and faith in our Creator God, who, we believe, loves us and all creation, and we expect that the course of nature will not alter. We believe that in the twinkle of an eye the Controller of the universe can reverse the order of nature and wipe out the various species of animals; yet we continue to hope that this will not happen. Even the reality of the killer disease AIDS cannot dampen our spirit. Our human ingenuity has now brought us to near calamity as we face the threat of annihilation or obliteration by nuclear interference, yet we are hopeful that the divine power, being the Super Power,

---

Lloyda Fanusie of Sierra Leone serves on the Commission on Faith and Order of the World Council of Churches. A lay preacher, she has a degree in Theology and is Supervisor of Family Life Education in Freetown, Sierra Leone.

will overcome the human power which is powerless in the presence of the divine power. We are thus encouraged to express our joy and expectations at the birth of every infant. Yet from the first moment, the various biases and determining factors begin to influence the individual in terms of who he or she is and what future roles are expected from that individual. From this perspective, we want to examine the role of religion in our lives with reference to human sexuality, giving a good deal of attention to female sexuality.

I shall consider the basic biological concept of the human physiognomy as an entry point. Science has gone a long way in helping us to understand what we once took for granted. Hereditary traits are clearly explained to us. Family resemblances of the eyes, voice, or other bodily features, the fact that a boy looks like his mother whereas a girl resembles her father, the fact that a child looks partly like both parents, or the straightforward cases of girl like mother and boy like father, are all explained by the combination of the $X + Y$ and $X + X$ chromosomes. The twenty-three chromosomes of the male sperm and the twenty-three of the female genes contain the DNA (deoxyribosenucleic acid) from which the human body develops. Yet we know that the child is not exactly like either parent, nor exactly like any other person in the world. I may look like my mother, but I am not my mother. Science has even made it possible for us to determine the sex of a child when a family is being planned; yet we must appreciate that each individual is unique, and we must live in obedience to God's will as we continue to reproduce and replenish the earth. Physical attributes on their own do not make up the entire nature of the individual. To understand the fully human person, we ought to consider other dimensions of his or her development. Accepting the fact that the "I and thou" relationship is a contributing factor to the wholeness of the individual, I would like to consider the fully human person as a being integrated in the social, spiritual, vocational, and physical dimensions.

Our social dimension encourages us to interact with other human beings, and we are able to rejoice with those who rejoice and weep with those who mourn. Our spiritual dimension ensures that we have the virtues of faith, hope, and love, as we relate to our neighbors and the God we worship. Life itself is seen as a gift from God, and this links us directly with God as individuals and collectively through religion. Our vocational dimension is that which encourages us to work in God's vineyard. Our work and lifestyle should be in obedience to God's will, as we care for all the worldly treasures under our control. Our physical attributes enable us to reproduce, and our features differentiate the male from female. No one dimension is of more importance than the others. In the sight of God, every aspect of creation is "good." From the human experiences of interaction in the realm of vocational, social, and cultural activities, as well as in the realm of religion, we see a different interpretation of what is "good." Religion is firmly rooted in the ethical values of community life, and all the members of the community relate to the supernatural power that has the good of the community at heart. The community consists of male and female members, and the psychosocial experience of male-female relationships are reflected in the spiritual sphere of their lives. This is perhaps why there is so much male dominance in questions of authority in religion.

A study of ancient religion gives a general impression that women were originally exalted, uplifted, and glorified. There is also evidence of feelings of ambivalence towards women, making them pure and virtuous on one hand, and on the other hand regarding them as polluted, unclean, and contagious. Traces of male dominance are also detected in contemporary religions, and although many of the world's religions were founded by men, for example, Jesus of Nazareth, Zoroaster, Mahavira, Gautama Buddah, Confucius, Nanak, Muhammad, and so forth, we cannot blame them, for there is evidence that the male dominance that exists in the religions developed gradually. In the process of being translated, the holy writings of some religions were misinterpreted, and this has resulted in women being relegated to the background as mere property, belonging to their fathers, brothers, and eventually their husbands. In widowhood, even their sons may continue the control system. In most religions, males wrote the codes, and when rituals were necessary, they were controlled by men. In like manner, men designed the laws and customs and, as would be expected, these were mostly to their favor and to the disadvantage of the women. It is our experience that the ancient myths of Africa and the Jewish and Christian myths have contributed immensely to the plight of women in Africa. Depending on the woman's docility or assertiveness, the myths portray the woman in two categories. If passive, she is noble, saintly and pure, and inspires man. If assertive, then she is evil, distracting man from his religious and worldly pursuits; she is a witch, a temptress, or a prostitute; and some myths even present her as a demon and symbol of sensual lust, a being whom man must fear. The Hebrew myth of Adam and Eve is structurally similar to many other tribal myths. Eve, the prototype of woman, is branded for bringing condemnation on the entire human species for eternity, because of her will to power and pursuit of knowledge.

In the Jewish and Christian view, woman is second to man in creation and status and the cause of the world's troubles. Due to her disobedience, Eve is punished accordingly (Gen. 3:16). Her pain in childbirth is increased, yet she will continue to lust for her husband who will rule over her. Several African myths portray the woman as being responsible for the rift between humankind and God. These myths depict God's transcendence, and they brand women as disobedient, greedy, curious, and self-centered. Indeed, the story of Pandora is retold in varied mythological accounts. Many of these myths are to be understood symbolically.

Two Yomba accounts refer to the greed and disrespect of a woman that deprived humankind of the unrestricted bliss of heaven. The oral traditions say that heaven was so near the earth that people could touch it. On one occasion, a greedy woman took a large quantity of food from heaven and could not finish it; as a result, heaven was removed from the reach of humankind, and the task of searching for food began. Another account tells that a woman with dirty hands touched the unsoiled face of heaven, and this led to our loss of heavenly bliss. An Akan account states that God and humankind lived close together, and God could be touched by all. An old woman used a mortar and pestle to pound her fufu, and each time she raised the pestle high enough to hit God, God moved farther and farther away from the earth until God went to the skies.

The woman and her colleagues attempted to bring God back to their midst by piling all the mortars one on top of another to form a ladder to reach God. When they needed just one more mortar, the woman suggested that they remove the first mortar at the bottom to put it on top. This was done, and the whole construction collapsed on them and many people were killed. Small wonder, then, that many ancient communities transferred these myths to real life and caused untold suffering for ill-fated women. In some cultures, some parents get rid of infant girls out of resentment. Their birth is seen as an ill omen to the men in such communities. Wisdom has saved the situation. Where would wives and mothers come from?

WOMEN AS A SOURCE OF POLLUTION

Survival of the fittest tends to result in male dominance. The concept of "pollution" and "contagion" in the religious sphere has been extended to human bodily secretions and excretions such as urine, blood, secretions from the genitals, and so forth, and regulations have been made in connection with such secretions and excretions for both the male and the female. There are laws regarding fornication, adultery, incest, sexual intercourse, and so forth, but apparently the female is victimized in their enforcement more often than the male. The woman is crushed more often; she faces more punitive measures than the man; and even in the case of restorative rituals, she has to undergo such rituals more often than the man. It is as if men are saying to women, "We are unclean, but you are more unclean than we are." In spite of her physical and mental fitness, a woman is usually excluded for her menstrual blood, her breast milk, and even for her ability to bear children. She is, therefore, unfit to touch holy vessels and dress in holy apparel—she cannot and must not "look" holy. These are male privileges that must be enjoyed by men only.

St. Paul, in his Letter to the Galatians, points out that what human nature wants is opposed to what the Spirit wants, and vice versa. Human nature shows itself in immoral, filthy, and indecent actions, as well as in idol worship and witchcraft, fighting, anger, jealousy, division, envy, drunkenness, and orgies. On the contrary, the Spirit produces love, joy, peace, patience, kindness, goodness, faithfulness, humility, and self-control. This is a warning to us to understand that in spite of the concept of original sin, which puts the female in a bad light, various forms of antisocial behavior unrelated to sex and lust can remove the individual from God's presence. In spite of the "holy look" and "holy apparel," there may be evidence of uncleanness of the mind which can disqualify those who claim to be clean from holding holy elements!

The many setbacks faced by women in Christianity are usually rooted in the Scriptures that, for the most part, are a heritage from the Jewish patriarchal system. Such attitudes have been taken for granted from the period of the early church and further confirmed by the sociocultural influences of developed communities that have embraced this religion and continued to misapply generic terms to promote male supremacy over female. Furthermore, when Christianity was introduced to African countries, it meant further male domination for females who were already experiencing unfair treatment in various spheres of their lives. The church needed women for moral and financial support, so they were welcomed into the spiritual fold with limitations. It reminds me of the Creole* expression, "Troway am nar beef—Eat am nar bone." Women were a necessary evil—throw them away—no! The church is unable to decide whether women are "bones" to be thrown away or "meat" to be eaten. There is indecision on how far women may be admitted as integral to the church.

While we ponder over this issue, let us recall the early Hebrew practice of rigid separation of men and women and the imposition of strict standards of modesty for the women. Men feared women's sexuality, and possibly the sight of a woman's body was enough to lead the male to lust. It was considered immoral, for example, for a Hebrew man to listen to a woman sing, to look at her hair, or to walk behind her in the street. Similar thoughts are expressed by other religious bodies. For example, in the Confucian Marriage Manual (sixth century

---

* Creole, also known as Krio, is a language group of West Africa.

B.C.E.), this description is given of women: "The five worst infirmities that afflict the females are indocility, ... discontent, slander, jealousy and silliness. Such is the stupidity of woman's character, that it is incumbent upon her, in every particular way, to distrust herself and to obey her husband." From the Hindu Code of Mann V (ca. 100 C.E.) we learn that "in childhood a woman must be subject to her father; in youth to her husband; when her husband is dead to her sons. A woman must never be free of subjugations." From the above points, we can appreciate that women face belittlement from all angles.

We sisters in Africa are no exceptions. We, too, come in for a full share of male domination! Our situation is worthy of note. In most areas, there is evidence of dualism in the religious experience of the people. In spite of the influence of the Christian and Islamic religions (which are dominant) and the gradual infiltration of other contemporary world religions into African communities, the adherence to traditional religious beliefs and practices is still rampant, and this imposes a double burden on the woman. She continues, like women in other parts of the world, to be someone's daughter, sister, wife, and mother. In many instances, she is blamed for many sexual inconsistencies in the human experience.

SEXUALITY AND PROCREATION

In general, the norm for male-female sexual relationships centers around marriage. People marry for the purpose of procreation. The Mende man in Sierra Leone, when asking for the hand of someone's daughter, would declare that he wants the person's daughter for "sex purposes." It is also generally asserted that humankind is heterosexual. This, when taken in its socioreligious setting, implies that within the sanctity of the marriage bond, a couple can procreate in fulfillment of God's will. If this is the norm, then, it follows that all extramarital relationships are frowned upon, and all sexual acts outside the heterosexual experience are taken as deviant sexual behavior. The punitive and restorative measures taken for such extramarital and deviant sexual activities vary from society to society, and in the majority of cases these activities are looked upon with repugnance. Yet we ought to reflect on certain practices and form realistic views about their acceptability or inacceptability. What have we to say about monosexual acts (masturbation) and male and female homosexuality? Are they cases of preference or determined by biological factors? Are these people freaks? Furthermore, what can we say about the conditions of impotence, sterility, impenetrable uterine membrane (known in vernacular as *Akriboto*), and the rare emergence of hermaphrodites? In many African settings, women were and are sometimes blamed for such conditions. A childless wife would be blamed, irrespective of the fact that her husband may be sterile or that she may be facing some health hazards.

SEX-RELATED TABOOS

Beliefs in homeopathic and contagious magic encourage the people to put a great premium on taboos related to their sexuality. During the period of puberty, a male experiencing "wet dreams" will believe that he is being bewitched by a female. Male potency may be dependent on the female in certain cases. If, for example, a man suffers from "blockage," he may attribute his condition to a female who has decided to punish him. A Mende woman will fill a bottle with her urine and bury it near a well or a river bank. She points out, when burying the bottle, that she has been meanly treated by the man, who failed to give her clothing, and so forth. As such, she puts a curse on the man that he will die by the bottle; the man is expected to die by uremia, unless she revokes the curse.

A taboo strongly adhered to by the Creoles is the one which states that a woman must not partake of her son's urine. If this should be disobeyed, the boy will become impotent (an *okobo*). Such a taboo will be adhered to, as no mother would like to be the cause of her son's impotence. Therefore, women take great care to watch the food they eat. They keep it away from a male infant in case the baby suddenly spurts urine. Mothers are particular about washing their hands after changing the wet baby. From the utilitarian point of view, one could see the rational behind the taboo in terms of proper hygiene, but it is given credence because no one wants to be a scapegoat.

A male child is also not to be flogged with a broom, as this would render him impotent. Here again one wonders what the relationship is between the broom and the penis. Sometimes a male can cause his own problems if he disobeys a taboo. For example, a male must not sit on top of a mortar. If he does so, he will suffer from elephantiasis of the scrotom. When a boy is suspected of coming out with protuding breasts during puberty, a pestle is used to "beat in" the female-like quality. But a female who shows a tendency to producing a beard will be branded a witch. Among some Creoles, girls were forbidden to climb a tree, as it was believed that the tree would become unproductive and eventually die. Is there something in the female genitals that is death-radiating? Some people still adhere to this taboo for fear that this is the case. Others prevent girls from climbing trees out of sex-role expectations.

The Ibos of Nigeria offer sacrifices to remove "abominations." These are classified into three types, two of which deal with women. Abomination embraces serious personal and moral crimes for the Ibos, and these include incest, willful abortion, and pregnancy within a year of the husband's death. Abomination also includes unusual, abnormal, and unnatural actions, such as giving birth to twins and abnormal presentation in the birth of a baby (for example, breech birth), and pounding the pestle on the ground instead of in the mortar while pounding fufu, even if by mistake. In all the above cases, a cleansing sacrifice is necessary to atone for the wrongdoer who eventually regains full association with the rest of the community.

In general, taboos on menstruating women are observed all over Africa. Women are considered unclean and are kept away from chiefs, they must not prepare food for chiefs, sometimes not even for their husbands and men going on business expeditions. Mostly the women are relegated to an outside hut or asked to keep away from areas where men are. In areas where gold is mined, they are restricted from going near the mines, as this would affect the mining activities adversely. The taboos are so many that they cannot all be considered in this article. Suffice it to say that whether they are simple restrictions regarding certain types of foodstuff or sterner measures against disrupting order and systems, they all share a common feature—the woman is ostracized for her "condition," and she accepts it as part of her lot in life that at certain times she is defiled.

The Creole trader who earns her living by petty trading in a product of beninseed called ogiri will never prepare this food while she is menstruating; the same is true of the woman who prepares "congoo" made out of peanuts. One wonders what the woman's bleeding has to do with the preparation of foodstuff for sale. But in actual fact, there could be a rationale behind such taboos, most of which are utilitarian. The preparation of certain foodstuffs takes time and energy, and if one is going through a period of bleeding, which symbolically means losing the essence of life, one might be unfit for such hazardous tasks and is therefore given the chance to rest until one returns to "normal."

The Mende believe that a woman will transmit bad luck to a male if coitus occurs when a woman is having her menses. At this time, a married woman is excused by her husband, who says she is busy and she has seen the moon. This implies that the wife is committed to a supernatural claim with which the husband must not compete. If a man has sexual intercourse with a widow, he will also have bad luck. The widow continues to be the property of the spirit of her deceased husband with full marital rights, until she has performed the required rites of purification after forty days. Sometimes taboos are placed on people for their own protection. One such is the taboo on a Sande initiate who has not completed the rites of the secret society. A man who violates her sexually will suffer the consequences of his action. No coitus will occur between a female and a male preparing to go out fishing, hunting, or gardening, for fear of failure in their endeavors.

The Mende and other people believe strongly that should coitus take place in a farm or bush, disaster will follow. The offspring of the couple will be dwarflike, and sometimes the farm will become unproductive until it is washed or cleansed of all defilement. In some cases, sexual intercourse is restricted to certain times of the day, and offenders are threatened with abdominal pain, sleeping sickness, sickly children, and sometimes death. Generally, sexual intercourse at odd times and in odd places is questioned, as it is seen as a deviant act. Why should a couple go to the farm or bush? Possibly they are having an illicit affair, as no married couple will indulge in such an act in the bush. Such a taboo reinforces the sanctity of marriage. In the case of wrong timing, possibly the act itself is considered debilitating or thought to induce sleep, so that a couple may find themselves sleeping or feeling drowsy when they are supposed to be alert, full of energy, and busy on their farm.

Several taboos relating to pregnancy are observed by women in the hope that they will eventually give birth successfully. They are seen as protective taboos for the benefit of mother and child. Sometimes educated women, as well as those belonging to the dominant religions, observe these taboos secretly and pretend that they are not involved. This is where we have evidence of dualism. Among my people, the Creoles, very few pregnant women will walk the streets at night without carrying a stone or penknife. Why? They are protecting themselves from evil spirits. A woman in such a condition must not walk unarmed in the night. Elderly women attribute deformity and abnormal behavior in infants and children to the possibility that the mother of such a child was strongheaded and disobeyed the taboo. Women are often warned to adhere to these taboos in spite of their attachment to "imported" religions. Obviously, such warnings coming from women indicate that it is the very women who promote and support these restrictions. Sometimes the men join them in the enforcement.

THE LOGIC OF TABOOS

Some African taboos might sound puzzling to someone from a country where issues are carefully analyzed, and people do not take things for granted. However, these taboos are meaningful for those who adhere to them, and when they are analyzed, a lot can be learned about the philosophy behind the people's thinking. Recently, I had the opportunity to hold discussions with some Mandingo teachers on male-female relationships. As would be expected, the rules are always in favor of men and against women. These rules may not be Islamic in origin, although the majority of the people are Muslims. You will note that the people accept male domination as a way of life, and even the educated ones find it hard to work against the system, even if they wish to do so.

The Mandingo man must not prepare food, sweep the house, or do any domestic chores if his wife is alive and living in the home. If he does, it is taken as an indication of weakness and ill-omen. The wife's life will be shortened. This, of course, is the crux of the matter. What woman would like to die for no just cause? Rather than die, the woman would work until she dies by "hard work." If a pregnant woman refuses to cook for her husband, it is believed that her child would eventually be a "cook." If a pregnant woman refuses to respond to her husband's call, the child will be born dumb. These are blatant evidence of attempts at obtaining subservience, couched in socioreligious constraints. I tried to reason this out with my friends, and we agreed that unless the present generation that propagates such ideologies "passes away," nothing much can be done in terms of reform. One woman told me of her attempts at the "parallel style of marriage." The mother-in-law could not understand why her son had to give his wife the salary he earned. She pressurized the young man, and he has stopped making decisions with his wife. Now they no longer have a common purse; he keeps his money and she keeps hers.

Still on the puzzling aspect of our taboos, I wish to consider two among the Creoles that relate to the potency of the female genitals. It is widely believed that a parrot should not see a naked woman. If it does, it will stop "speaking" and eventually die. This is a belief which has passed on from one generation to the next, and stories have been told about the reason for this bird's fate. The woman originally put a curse on the parrot for reporting her infidelity to her husband. She might have sworn by her genitals. Whatever the case, we have before us what we might call a "myth of evil." There are instances when I have heard of women stripping themselves naked to put a curse on their children. These are very rare, as it is strongly believed that such a curse cannot be revoked. For a mother to reach such a decision means that the child must have gone to extremes in his or her behavior towards the mother.

One thing which strikes me is the importance attached to the female genitals. On the one hand, people are apologetic if they have cause to refer to the genitals, and on the other hand, they heap abuses on each other by reference to the female and sometimes male genitals when quarreling. From childhood, one is trained to understand the human genitals as areas of obscenity. If a child uses a word in the vernacular to refer to the genitals, he or she has to apologize for using a "bad word" or obscene language. When someone abuses another's mother in terms of the genitals, the latter becomes so incensed that he or she might even become violent. It is interesting to note that more abuses are uttered against mothers than against fathers, and I wonder why this is so when we esteem the mothers very highly, to the extent that we cannot accommodate abusive language against them.

The second taboo relates to infants. Two infants must not smile at each other. If this happens, they will become dumb. This sounds unrealistic until we stop and consider its implications. The sanction of this taboo will further clarify its value. The mothers of the infants who have smiled to each other have to "redeem" their children by a ritual of exposure. They have to run naked around the house where the incident occurred, each starting in the opposite direction and crossing each other on the way. This is a very serious matter with the Creoles, and great care is taken by nursing mothers to ensure that their babies do not come into close contact with other babies. The thought of running naked will make one think twice about being careless in such a matter. For two infants to smile at each other, they must be in close proximity. At once we can deduce that such closeness might lead to infection. There is a medical hazard which must be avoided, as the babies' immunity would be low. Thus, on medical grounds, the taboo serves a purpose. What of mothers running naked? It would be a check on them to avoid being careless. The punishment for carelessness is exposure of the genitals, from whence the process of conception started that eventually led to the production of a child through the same source. I am still trying to unravel the mystery behind this taboo, which also can be seen as a way of belittling and humiliating women. One might decide not to observe this taboo, yet no mother would want her child to be dumb, and so she will subject herself to the ritual if she allows her child to come into close contact with another infant.

TOUCHY ISSUES

I cannot complete my examples of African reflections on human sexuality without dealing with a few cases of incest. This varies from one ethnic group to the next. Some are specific on blood ties; others extend it to in-laws as well. At times, the law of incest is extended to physical associations like shaking the hands of those within the prohibition. Punitive and restorative measures vary, but two very harsh types have to be discussed. Among the Temnes, if two sisters have intercourse with the same man, a dog is cooked and the culprits have to eat part of the meat. The Sherbros also use a dog for their cleansing ritual. The culprits will run along a path leading to a stream or pool. People line the route holding whips that they use to flog the culprits. When they reach the pool, a dog is slaughtered and its blood drained into the water. The culprits then bathe in the water before further rituals are performed. In both examples, we note that the culprits have been linked with dogs. Their incestuous act is associated with dogs. These rituals make a substitution sacrifice by the slaughter of a dog.

I have decided to deal with a very "touchy" topic as my final consideration. This is the current debate about female circumcision. This practice is still supported by women. Westernized countries have banned it, although one is not certain of what happens behind locked doors unknown to the authorities. This is a burning issue which cannot be dismissed. At the same time, one wonders how to approach it. Most Creoles do not practice it, and if someone who is not directly involved makes condemnatory statements, others might see it as interference.

There are other areas in which I dream of change, but my dreams remain unexpressed, as I am certain I will be branded as being tribalistic, or I might even find myself excommunicated for being heretical. But one wish which I can express is this: I wish I had a whip, just like the one Jesus used when he overturned the tables of the money changers and later flogged them. Indeed, I wish I had a whip!

The Limba of Sierra Leone place such a premium on female virginity that at marriage, if the bride is virtuous, the relatives of the husband will take with them a white kolanut to present to the parents of the bride. If she is not, then a red kolanut is sent as a sign of disgrace. In an ancient Creole custom, women carried the white bedspread with the blood stains along the road, singing, "Hot corn tiday broke oh!," meaning that the hot corn (symbolizing the hymen) has been broken today. These very ancient stringent measures on "spoiled" females are now being overlooked. This does not mean that licentious and frivolous living is being advocated. To be a virgin at marriage is still considered the ideal.

Should not men, too, be subjected to the demands of virginity and fidelity in marriage? Even as married women, females are sexually harassed. For example, some tribes accept the husband's right to give one of the wives in his harem to visitors who are on a long journey. At times, if the man has gone hunting or on a long journey, his brother was permitted to enjoy the rights and privileges of a husband with the wife at home. So women can be declared as objects of sex from that perspective. Women are also victims of rape, and sometimes they are blamed for inviting the men through their actions or by the way they move. When they are waylaid in dark places, the men have excuses — they have sexual urges that cannot be controlled.

Another area to consider is that of prostitution. This is a problem, for some women become prostitutes out of need. Others become prostitutes due to male pressures. The women are branded and looked down upon, but no one questions the men who interact with them. Prostitution is still looked upon as something which bad women do. As such, even those in authority come down hard on the women, chasing them about and punishing them. In religious thinking, the practice of prostitution is a sin. In the Old Testament, Israel is often referred to as a prostitute, straying from Yahweh and following other "lovers." Israel then is termed "she." My question with regards to prostitution is: Why the different measuring rod? If the "sellers" are branded, why not the "buyers"?

In my discussions with some men, I learned that they see men as "sufferers" in cases of adultery, because, according to traditional custom, they have to pay the fine. In traditional society, women name the names of men with whom they have had extramarital affairs, and the husbands, after hearing such confessions, summon the culprits to the chief who will then levy fines on the men. Adultery takes place predominantly in polygamous homes in which the husbands are not able to satisfy the sexual needs of their wives because they are too busy or too old. In monogamous homes, an angry and jealous husband can even hack an adulterous wife to death. As I considered the views of my friends, I pointed out to them that there was more to the fine-paying than can be easily grasped at first sight. Here is evidence of a husband preserving his marital rights as well as giving the other men, who are usually unattached, the opportunity to satisfy their sexual urges. Thus, one can see how men capitalize on their wives' adultery, receiving fines from the culprits. This is a covert form of exploitation of the women.

When men commit adultery, the wives are not compensated from fines levied on the female culprit. In some cases in which wives complain of their husband's adultery, they are given gifts to coax them and to soften their hearts. The husbands usually expect forgiveness, as they see their action as a male privilege. As regards marital rights, the stress is more on the demands made on the woman. The male sexual urge must be fulfilled. Fidelity on the part of females is a must. At the onset of marriage, females face pressure as males stress the importance of virginity. Why only the female? Should not the male be virtuous? In most cases, if a marriage is to be dissolved for disrespect, disobedience, childlessness, or other reasons, it is usually the wife who suffers. Sometimes she runs away from home as a result of ill treatment by her husband. Sometimes the husband sends her away to her parents, and if he can prove that she is in the wrong, he calls for a return of the "bride-price." So we see that, whatever the situation, the woman is on the losing end.

Thus, we can clearly conjecture that when the nurse or doctor or midwife makes the announcement that "it is a boy," the parents and all supporters are gleeful as they see all avenues open before him. He will mature in all dimensions and will find fulfillment in whatever role he wants to perform. For him the sky is the limit! When the announcement is made that "it is a girl," the news is received differently. The possibilities are there, but there is a big "but." The limitations are many; the expectations are fixed. She will end up as a wife and mother, obediently cooking for her family and finding fulfillment in this as a major role, while she finds other minor interests to engage her during what spare moments these leave her. Indeed, the male is there to give "pregnancy" to the female (even if he is sterile). The female is there to "receive" pregnancy, and if she fails to do so, she is branded. She is there to serve the male, to satisfy his desires irrespective of her many potentials.

SOME CONCLUSIONS

I am quite aware of the fact that I am not a "highly qualified" theologian, but I know that God has endowed me with a "thinking faculty," and I am able to reflect on issues pertaining to myself and other females of the human species. My views may sound naive and nonempirical, yet I am certain that the points I have raised are worthy of note. It is high time that we begin to accept the beauty of nature's diversity and see the work of God as "good." We must appreciate the gift of life, a precious gift that humanity cannot create. In spite of our human gifts of ingenuity and knowledge, we still continue to propagate theories which only end in "confusion" as others come up with queries which do not apply to such theories. I see this as a warning! Let us reflect on the biblical account of the Tower of Babel and take our cue. We expound on the theories of "the battle of the sexes." The male is dominant and "superior." The female has innate strength which the male fears and of which he is jealous. The mysterious birthgiving ability of the females and their tie to nature and fertility is another source of male fear and jealousy. The female avoids dangerous situations for the purpose of gestation and nursing, which limits their participation in such activities as hunting, fighting in wars, and so forth. The male revolts against matriarchal societies, and gets revenge for his former status of inferiority in such societies by attempting to dominate the female species in all aspects of life.

Women have come out with new concepts like androgyny and unisex, terminologies like "inclusive language" and "feminist science." We worry a lot about the misconceptions and misinterpretation of generic terms in scriptural accounts; and the more we unearth these problems, the more confused we become, and we refuse to see the simple reality of nature. Even the word "nature" poses a problem, as its implications are debated by many scholars! My appeal to you is to avoid skirting the issues, avoid shelving and actually delve into reality. Let us accept the fact that we are a species, male and female, each with special blessings and functions for the well-being and wholeness of humanity. As Christians, let us accept with seriousness the bold claim that we are created in the image and likeness of God. Neither the male nor the female of our species is superior to the other. We can accept the variety of our endowments and try to unite in spite of our differences.

We need to reorient our thinking about limitations which have been and are being determined by human beings. We should reflect on God's unity and plurality and relate this to ourselves who are in God's image and likeness, a community of male and female with inherent qualities as well as qualities derived from our environment. The God we worship is, in essence, the one-in-three and three-in-one God; the unchanging Father—our Creator, Son-Redeemer and Spirit-Sanctifier. In God's image and likeness, we need not and we ought not to change our being. We need not interfere with nature by reconditioning our hormones and attempting to "correct" nature. We might reach a certain point in our scientific prowess, but I am certain we will eventually come to a standstill. We shall forever witness the wonder of procreation. A woman will menstruate and give birth; a man will not. A woman will produce a son looking like herself, she will produce a daughter looking like the father. A woman will produce a child looking like a combination of herself and the father of the child. These are basic human experiences which we cannot evade.

As regards sexuality and religion, we have an opportunity to reconsider our concepts of pollution and contagion. We can relate them to the divine plan and see if they have a part in it. Because of our sexuality, we women have suffered from discrimination and disservice, and sometimes we are tempted to feel that we have been born the wrong sex. But we cannot sit back and continue to wallow in dismay as we ponder over our "lot" as women. How long can we continue to serve as supportive "better halves" of the male species? How long will we be identified as the nurturing mother, the child bearer, the loving wife, caretaker, and security officer of the home, affiliated to the male species and also vulnerable to its whims and fancies? How long will we continue as burden bearers, hewers of wood, and drawers of water, the touched yet untouchable, in need of ceremonial cleanings, subjected to bathings and washings by male purifiers and prayermen? How long will we sit back as lookers-on in a religious congregation during worship? How long will we continue to stand aside and defer to our men even when the means of grace is being distributed? We have been branded for so long; should this continue?

We have a problem. We see the marks of discrimination—we are sometimes mutilated in the name of culture and religion. These things are happening in real life. We know the root causes—sometimes misinterpretation of Scripture, sometimes ignorance, sometimes selfishness, sometimes bossiness. Our challenge now is, what can we do about the situation? I am certain that many suggestions will be given. In the world of work, women have begun to make themselves felt and respected. In the world of science, women are involved in discussing our sexuality. In the psychosocial arena, we are quite active in making the male aware of our human strengths and weaknesses. We want to share and share alike. I expect that in the religious arena, we too should continue to create an awareness in the minds of our counterparts. I know this will take some time, but I know it will happen. The big change will surely come, and we shall with one accord sing praises to our God and King. We have a lot of work to do in terms of study and empowerment. How do we go about reversing old concepts, "unsaying" what has been said? We need studies that will demonstrate the mutual responsibility for the evils of society. We need to get men

n taking a more scientific approach to male impotence
r male inadequacies that are attributed to female
nce. Women are as human as men. So it is together
that we should seek and work for the good of the human community.

REFERENCES

Arinze, Francis A. *Sacrifice in Iboland.* Ibadan University Press, 1970.
Birke, Lynda. *Women, Feminism and Biology.* New York: Menthen Inc.,
    1986.
Finnegan, R. H. *Survey of the Limba People of Northern Sierra Leone.*
    London: Her Majesty's Stationery Office, 1965.
Freeman, Joe. *The Politics of Woman's Liberation.* New York: David
    Mckay Company Inc., 1975.
Harris, W. T., and Harry Sawyer. *The Springs of Mende Belief and Con-
    duct.* Freetown: Sierra Leone University Press, 1968.
Opoku, Kofi Asare. *West African Traditional Religion.* FEP International
    Private Ltd., 1978.

10

Human Sexuality, Marriage, and Prostitution

Bernadette Mbuy Beya

The implications of sexuality in our African culture make it anything but comfortable for us to address this topic. In our culture, the subject is taboo. Despite the difficulties, however, some of us African women are determined to study this matter in depth. After all, sexuality is a prime factor in the determination of behavioral reality, both of human beings in general and of women in particular. Our profoundly spiritual and realistic investigations demonstrate that the problem of sexuality is one that concerns us all. The exercise of sexuality is altogether subject to a woman's freedom and hence is her responsibility.

Over the course of a year, a group of fifteen women under the presidency of Sister Marie Bernadette Mbuy Beya conducted personal observations, field investigations, and read selected works. Our research describes the development of sexuality in African women, emphasizing the sexual awakening in

Translated from French by Robert R. Barr.

Bernadette Mbuy Beya, a religious sister from Zaire, is Mother Superior of the Ursuline Sisters and Director of the Institut Supérieur des Sciences Réligieuses in Lubumbashi, Zaire. She studied at the Institut des Sciences Réligieuses (Lumen Vitae) in Brussels, Belgium.

girls and adult women. Next, we consider the matter of conjugal fidelity, basing our reflections on the actual practices of certain tribes in Zaire such as the Bena Lulua and Baluba of Kasai, the Bandibu, the Bantandu of Lower Zaire, and the Tshokwe of Shaba.

We then present a succinct analysis of the situation of the unmarried woman in African society, the psychological and cultural implications of being unmarried, and the difficulties of this state of life. Next, we analyze the causes and consequences of prostitution, in light of data collected in our interviews with a sample of twenty women from among the approximately two hundred prostitutes working in the city of Lubumbashi. Finally, we attempt to establish the relationship between sexuality and religion in terms of African cultural values and the conception of sexuality maintained by the Catholic church.

Our description of sexuality will be presented in terms of the experience of African women in general and Zairian women in particular. Although women's sexuality obviously cannot be examined in isolation from that of men, given the objectives of the present study we shall deal here explicitly only with the sexual behavior of women.

DEVELOPMENT OF SEXUALITY IN AFRICAN WOMEN

As we do not propose to enter upon any theoretical consideration of sexuality, we shall need only a working definition: sexuality is the ensemble of activities by which human beings seek and attain the satisfaction of their sexual inclinations. At once we encounter an obstacle: the delicacy of the African attitude toward sexuality. Our traditional behavior and customs include a whole series of sexual initiatory practices, it is true; but it is regarded as immodest to speak of them in public.

It is in terms of this African, and more precisely Zairian, sociocultural world that we shall endeavor to convey an understanding of women's sexual behavior. Of course, Africa has arrived at its present state along a complexity of historical paths. Thus, the practices and initiations to which we shall be referring are not identical in every respect throughout the continent.

Their difference in form, however, does not belie their basic similarity.

Women's sexuality is far more diffuse and gradual in its development than that of the opposite sex. A woman's splendid, lissome body functions as a powerful element of erotic attraction for men. African women's initiation in sexuality, while never omitted, is implemented with discretion. An African woman makes no overt effort to exhibit her sexual qualities or tendencies. She prefers to have these merely surmised—in her posture, her gait, or, for example, her proficiency in the execution of certain traditional dances.

Africans undergo their initiation between the ages of ten and twenty. The procedure differs according to gender. In each case, however, all concerns converge upon a single finality: the union of the sexes. Girls' sexual activities are regarded as of capital importance. A girl, it is said, should come to her marriage a "perfect woman," in affective, relational, as well as sexual terms. From the first day of her marriage, a girl will be expected to meet all of the conditions required by society.

In traditional societies, a girl's upbringing in sexuality, while inconspicuous, was very harsh and very strictly regulated. These activities were all the more important for her in that she risked remaining single for life unless her upbringing had been seen to in suitable fashion. A failure here meant shame, of course, for the entire family; but also, and especially, it was devastating for the personality of the ostracized girl.

These activities to prepare a girl to assume her marriage role as wife in a worthy manner began the moment her first menses announced the onset of puberty. Menstruation, that token of her future motherhood, was looked upon as a kind of sign of the reliability of her body, and she would now profit from an adequate sexual education. Thus, a girl's sexual preparation progresses from her definition as a female to a determination of her future attitudes as the partner in a marriage.

In many tribes, a girl who has lost her virginity before marriage has a grievous burden of guilt to bear—indeed, one that she might have to bear all her life.[1] In fact, in some African lands her initiation would now include a clitoridectomy, with the intent of preventing her from experiencing sexual pleasure and thus possibly from succumbing to the temptation of adultery after her marriage.

Marriage is regarded as the sovereign social regulator of sexuality. Marriage is the union of persons of opposite sexes for the purpose of the procreation and rearing of the human species. But while society decrees that the purpose of conjugal life is both the fertility and the pleasure of the couple, the female partner plays only a passive role. She must not seek her own sexual gratification. Indeed, a woman who becomes sexually aroused may not, as a rule, directly invite her partner to sexual pleasure. In doing so she would seem too sensually inclined, and thus vulnerable to the temptations of misconduct and adultery.

A woman's sexuality transcends her intimate relations with her partner and embraces the entire area of their relationship. It orientates a woman's intimate personal being toward a conjugal equilibrium and the compatibility of both partners. Woman is regarded as the generator of life. She is the mother of the children, the mother of everyone. By her motherhood, she establishes her status in society, and ensures the demographic growth of the group. And she is mightily proud of it. Thanks to her status as a mother, she succeeds in maintaining a balanced personality in her sexual life.

CONJUGAL FIDELITY

The word "fidelity" is heard very frequently in African speech. Daily, women and men pledge each other their "fidelity." But it is difficult to settle upon a universal definition for the word — all the more in that, for example, among certain tribes, like the Tshokwe of Zaire, a bridegroom selects one intimate friend of his to have sexual relations with his wife whenever he is away. Nor is his wife thought of as being unfaithful to him in having sexual relations with his surrogate. Thus, the concept of conjugal fidelity is one of great complexity. However, *Petit Robert* defines fidelity as not ignoring or neglecting one's commitments, while *Larousse* defines it as the quality of a person who abides by his or her commitments, who manifests a constant devotion, and who has relations only with his or her partner.

The law prescribes conjugal fidelity with a view to protecting the institution of marriage. Thus, civil law has sanctioned monogamous marriage in order to require spouses to maintain fidelity with each other. In Zaire, this regulatory function includes a "Family Code," which stipulates in Article 459 that spouses owe each other "fidelity."[2] The Penal Code conceives adultery as the sexual union of a married person with someone other than his or her spouse. Sanctions are provided in the case of any act that would be injurious to the family, especially the abandonment of the conjugal roof, adultery, and abortion.

A flagrant injustice appears, however, when it comes to punishing the infidelity of men and women respectively. Fidelity is far more rigorously required of a wife than of a husband. Adultery on the part of the latter is punishable only in the presence of aggravating circumstances, such as the introduction of his concubine into the marriage bed.

Fidelity as defined here by dictionaries and law fails to take account of certain more profound aspects of the sacred union of the married couple. One ought to be faithful not only in deed, but also in thought. When this second element is neglected or absent, grave disturbances ensue in the affective and social behavior of the spouses. Although psychotherapists encounter these cases on a daily basis, traditional societies have not waited for the elaboration of legal texts before exorcising these disturbances ritually (as we shall see below).

Zaire's 365 cultures[3] have different views of a girl's premarital sexuality and a married woman's fidelity. But we shall follow Kinyamba Shomba's grouping of these various attitudes in three categories: strict observance, indifference, and aversion.[4]

Societies of strict observance are inflexible when it comes to a young girl's virginity or a wife's fidelity. This is the case, for example, among the Luba and the Bena Lulua of the two Kasais, as in certain subgroups of the Bakongo (the Bantandu and the Bandibu). In these societies, sexual morality is regarded as being of paramount importance, and a woman's infidelity is severely punished. A girl who is not a virgin cannot marry with honor. If, by reason of attenuating circumstances, she manages to marry at all, both families concerned must be informed, and the mother of the bride will not receive the "virginity gift."

Infidelity on the part of a wife is strictly proscribed, as it is regarded as a threat to public morals and traditions. The mother of the delinquent wife is regarded as the main culprit: her daughter's act is palpable evidence of a poor upbringing. Among the Luba of both Kasais, an adulterous wife exposes her husband, her children, and herself to serious danger. It is thought that the most reasonable thing to do with her, then, is to send her home to her parents. If for some reason her husband prefers to keep her, she must submit to the rite of purification. This generally includes physical torture and social and economic sanctions, with certain tribal variations. Her husband's sisters, along with several other women, beat her, spread her thighs and force pepper or earth into her genitals. They may tie her arms and lay her in a hut on a lath floor, then light a fire into which they cast pepper so that the smoke may cause her more suffering. In the economic domain, the offended husband hires brigands to destroy the fields of the members of his wife's family or those of her lover. After the torture, the family of the adulteress is obliged to provide some kind of compensation.

Peoples in Zaire indifferent to or antipathetic to virginity in girls and fidelity in women are notably the Otetela, the Bakete, and the Babindji in Kasai, and the Basanga and the Bayeke in Shaba. Here adultery is not a cause for divorce, especially if the wife's relations are somehow beneficial to the couple. For example, a woman who owns a small business, or the wife of a man who owns such a business, may have sexual relations with men whose favor may improve her family's economic and social condition. Then too, that a woman is desired by men other than her husband is evidence of her beauty and power of attraction. Indeed, in these societies, a girl must be "completely" prepared for marriage—first by her aunts as far as theory is concerned, then by a man other than her prospective bridegroom for the the sake of practical skills.

A number of factors are favorable to fidelity on the part of the wife:

1. Before marriage:
   - Parents who are faithful, virtuous, sober, open and available, responsible, at least minimally well-off financially
   - A religion of high moral standards

2. After marriage:
   - A husband who is faithful, religious, with an employment not requiring prolonged absences, relatively easy-going, in good health, sexually normal, a responsible, protecting friend, lover, and brother
   - A united family
   - Friends capable of giving good advice
   - Good hygiene

Factors unfavorable to fidelity on the part of the wife include:

1. Before marriage
   - Unfaithful parents
   - Religious indifference
   - Careless upbringing
   - Bad neighborhood (for example, near a club or tavern)
   - Poor financial means
   - Permissive mores
   - Consumer society
2. After marriage:
   - Physical abuse
   - Jealousy
   - Revenge
   - Bad company
   - Overworked husband
   - Childlessness
   - Frustration
   - Lack of trust

Factors favorable to fidelity on the part of the husband include that the wife should be a good housekeeper, pleasant with her husband, calm, watchful of her figure, careful about spacing her pregnancies, a good manager of the family and the family budget, respectful of tradition, capable of portioning out her affection between her husband and her children, careful about her hygiene.

The consequences of infidelity are breakup of the marriage, the family, and society; psychological disturbances in the children and juvenile delinquency; withdrawal from the sacraments; venereal disease or AIDS; religious fetishism; psychosomatic illnesses; suicide; homicide. Infidelity on the part of the husband leads to diminished economic resources, seclusion, and loneliness.

If all of these disasters are to be avoided, mutual understanding will have to prevail. All of the favorable factors cited above ought to be taken into consideration, and instilled from childhood onward. We suggest that couples make an effort to practice a certain discernment: in marriage, as elsewhere, the ideal is often not the reality. The partner whom one is ready to betray is not necessarily a worse mate than the person newly desired. One must be prepared to make certain concessions, and to tolerate certain whims and demands. After all: "Lovers are not always face to face. Sometimes they are side by side" (Saint-Exupéry).

In the case of those who agree with the capital importance of marital fidelity, and who have considered the consequences of deviations from this sacred ideal, we should simply ask them to bring up their children in this same ideal. But we think that a conversion of mentality is in order when it comes to penalties imposed on women, especially on an unfaithful wife. The law of complete, sincere forgiveness ought to apply. Husbands should assist their fallen spouses to rise up again. They should also help them avoid dangerous occasions. "Let anyone among you who is without sin be the first to throw a stone at her," Jesus said (John 8:7). As for those who attach no importance to marital fidelity, we point to the deleterious effect of such behavior on home and family.

Ideally, husband and wife ought to be "one flesh" (Matt. 19:6). If we may express a further wish, it is that the fidelity of the couple be the concern of the two partners, and not merely of their families. And if today's society is to become more just, corrective measures must be applied in the case of infidelity on a husband's part as well, and not only in the case of the unfaithful wife.

AFRICAN WOMEN AND SINGLE LIFE

In the past, in certain African populations, only particular individuals selected to perform particular social functions remained unmarried. Among these individuals, some had been "eunuchs who have been so from birth," of whom the clan was very much ashamed. There was great concern that a man be able to engender children. Unmarried women, on the other hand, seem on the whole to have been accepted in our traditional societies, and integrated into them. Today, the ranks of unmarried women are swelling by leaps and bounds. For better or for worse, being married has become part of the story of African woman.

Nowhere in Africa does the law provide for the protection of unmarried women. When these women are asked to express themselves, then, or to make their own decisions about their lives, they are uncomfortable. After all, their society is ruled by the "marvelous" legislation of the male! When they attempt to define their situation, their natural sensitivity readily inclines them to spiritualize it, or to allege sentimental or economic reasons for it. Their unmarried state of life wins them no respect from others.

For purposes of this essay, we shall limit ourselves to presenting a brief analysis of the notion of celibacy (used here in a secular rather than a religious sense) in African society, with its various forms and characteristics; then we shall indicate some of the implications of this reality; finally, we shall suggest certain approaches that might be taken to some of the problems.

The dictionary (in French) defines celibacy as the state of an unmarried person. Simone de Beauvoir[5] appeals to this definition in order to demonstrate that a single woman is defined as a woman not invested with the dignity of a married one. This summary definition is not far from the thinking of the African of yesterday.

In Zaire, among the Songye, a single woman is variously referred to as *Mulungantu* — a respectable unmarried woman designated by the clan for certain political and spiritual functions; or *Kitesha* — a woman abnormal from birth, who is often concealed from the public and who is regarded in practice as an imbecile or cretin.

Among the Baluba of Kasai, she is called a *Mukaji mujika* — a woman living alone, a single woman, but this term has a different meaning than the so-called *ndumba*, or prostitute.

Among the Baluba of Mutombo Mukulu, a celibate female

may be chosen to perform a royal function. Such a woman is called the *Ndalamba* — the spiritual mother of the chief, charged with the maintenance of the sacred perpetual fire. She may no longer work outside the royal enclosure. Her role is to maintain this fire, invoke the spirits of the ancestors when the kingdom finds itself in difficulty (epidemic, war, etc.), counsel the chief, and bless his journeys.

Among the Baluba of Kabongo, there was another sacred or ritual celibacy, this time connected with the initiation of young girls. This woman was called the *Inabatanda* — the mother of the virgins, of the uninitiated. She was a well-bred, well-educated woman, selected by the chief expressly to take charge of the initiation of girls. She might also discreetly respond to the advances of the king, without, however, becoming pregnant, in which case she was dismissed.

Among the Arund of Shaba, an unmarried woman has the name of *Ruwej*, the female Lunda "chief," whose celibacy is imposed by her royal function. She is not permitted to have children, although she is known to be allowed to select a man for the discreet satisfaction of her sexual needs.

Again, in the region of Maniema in Zaire there is a form of celibacy bound up with initiatory functions. The woman holding this office is called the *Mwali*. She is a woman of good character, charged with the upbringing of girls and their preparation for marriage.

Thanks to contact with other cultures, and to Christian evangelization, a consecrated celibacy has come into existence in Africa that defines itself as a gift of God: a special consecration to God and to one's brothers and sisters for the purpose of bringing them salvation and bearing witness to the values of the world to come.

The various forms of celibacy just presented will afford the reader a glimpse of the diversity of the concept, as well as of the functions assigned to celibacy in ancient African society, where a certain harmony of life and relationships reigned. One might say that unmarried women were acknowledged and respected. But we wonder whether this ancient understanding of single women has been integrated into the Africa of today.

IMPLICATIONS OF SINGLE WOMEN TODAY

Being unmarried today has three different forms of implications for African women: psychological, economic, and cultural.

Psychological Implications. The unmarried African woman, no longer feeling accepted, but only tolerated, lives in a state of continual tension, and seeks at all costs to be protected by someone, even at the price of wresting the latter from his own family. This drama sometimes leads to suicide, or to certain illnesses like neurosis, depression, hypertension, gastritis, and so on, or to certain sexual deviations like masturbation or prostitution.

Economic Implications. The African woman is accustomed to being maintained by a man. Today she finds herself in a society of increasing poverty, in which one person can no longer see to the needs of many other persons. Thus, an unemployed single woman sees herself condemned to a life of material mediocrity. And so she is tempted to turn to prostitution.

The low standard of living of our various populations impels certain African religious women whose parents are very poor to assist their families by means of gifts obtained outside of the community. This sometimes leads to their compromising themselves sexually with their benefactors and abandoning the religious life.

Cultural Implications. While being unmarried is tolerated in Africa, childlessness (apart from ritual celibacy) is definitely not. Hence the proliferation of single motherhood. But how can a mother suitably rear these children of different fathers whom the clans are no longer willing to support? The single mother's situation often obliges her to undertake hard work outside the home in order to be able to rear her children.

The African religious woman often feels deprived in not having had children, when her whole basic upbringing has been oriented to motherhood. The mixed cultural world in which she is called to toil poses problems for her when it comes to maintaining fidelity to her life ideal.

How can single women be integrated into today's African society? The question is a recurring one. Answers are difficult to find, to formulate, and to have accepted. As long as women continue to be regarded as objects of pleasure and a capital resource, it will be difficult to integrate unmarried women into the society, and have their lifestyle accepted as a legitimate, in fact positive and expansive, lifestyle. Meanwhile, however, an ideal situation ought at least to be presented, even if its realization might never come about.

There is an urgent need for laws for the protection or rescue of the single female, and for the education of men to accept women as equal partners who deserve esteem and respect and with whom men can collaborate in the construction of a better world.

Consecrated celibacy should be encouraged. It should be seen as the vehicle of certain typically African spiritual values—values necessary in any society hoping to achieve a harmonious inner functioning.

Finally the church should pursue its task in working for the liberation of women, by way of open and forthright promotion of the interests of single women in particular.

AFRICAN WOMEN AND PROSTITUTION

In our work to analyze the situation of African women we found it imperative to ask women themselves to speak out, and to tell us what they experience as women and what routes to liberation they propose. What we had in mind was an attempt, on the one hand, to describe prostitution as practiced in the south of Zaire, more precisely in the city of Lubumbashi, and at the same time to come to grips with some of the consequences of this phenomenon for the lives of women and of the entire population.

And so we undertook to interview a score, or some 10 percent, of the approximately two hundred prostitutes working in Lubumbashi. The interviews we conducted represent some forty hours of listening and questioning, and the meaningful results obtained contain an enormous amount of data to be interpreted. The main thing we learned from them is that the imprisoned heart of the prostitute yearns for deliverance.

In the light of the data collected in the course of this field work and notwithstanding our personal discomfort as interviewers, we perceive no human value in prostitution. The reason is that in prostitution, sexual relations that ought to be understood in terms of a union of love between spouses and an openness to procreation, in fidelity and shared responsibility, are replaced by a mere mercenary service. In Zairian Bantu languages, including Swahili, a prostitute is called a *ndumba*. The term designates not only a woman who bestows her body in exchange for some material consideration, but any woman or man who submits to a multiplicity of partners.

The prostitutes with whom we met explained that while prostitution as a line of work is beset with certain risks, it is generally well remunerated. There is also "occasional" prostitution practiced by girls and young women with their teachers, but these girls and women do not become attached to prostitution, ashamed as they are of their practices. Despite our reticence to express any censure of the practices being described, the prostitutes themselves condemned them. Most burst into tears at their own picture of the basis of their moral misery.

Causes of Prostitution

The causes of prostitution are manifold. They may be linked to the person herself or may be dictated by the economic situation of her family. Of the twenty women whom we interviewed, two seemed relatively happy and content with their way of life, even though they had originally been thrust into it by circumstances. The following causes were cited.

1. Lack of affection.

2. Parental unemployment and destitution. It is not unusual to find parents who send their daughter into the street in order to be able to feed the family.

3. An unfaithful or polygamous husband. An unfaithful husband has so many women to maintain that a wife and children may be left to their own devices. In order that the family may have a decent living, the wife feels compelled to make use of the last resource at her disposition: her body.

4. Wife-abuse. An abused, battered wife, compelled to flee her husband, often has no other recourse if she hopes to support herself.

5. Lack of sexual information. Many girls, even those with some schooling, are not adequately instructed by their parents or teachers. A mother may ignore her daughter's menstrual periods, with enormous consequences for the adolescent.

6. "Operation Minerva." This term applies to the prostitution of schoolgirls and college students who must work their way through school. There is also another form of prostitution that occurs in connection with schooling. At times it takes on alarming proportions, even in religious institutions and often results from the sexual harassment of female students by their teachers.

Of the twenty prostitutes we interviewed, four turned to prostitution between fifteen and twenty years of age, eight began between twenty and thirty, and the remaining eight became prostitutes between thirty and forty years of age. In describing why they turned to prostitution, only two women mentioned a desire for adventure. The remaining eighteen became prostitutes because of material or emotional poverty, and prostitution was suggested to them by a female friend. Of these eighteen, ten were physically abused or divorced women, five had parents who had died and/or were working their way through school, one was an abandoned orphan, and two women were daughters of prostitutes.

In sum, we must say that the great general cause of prostitution is the abject poverty in which most of the families of the prostitutes are forced to live.

Consequences of Prostitution

1. Illness. All of the prostitutes interviewed carry condoms, but many of their clients are in too much of a hurry to be willing to use them. And clients who have contracted a sexually transmitted disease are eager to make victims of the prostitutes they later frequent. These prostitutes know, then, that they are at risk, and speak of the "hazards of the work." At the same time, they are aware that a sexually transmitted disease will be very costly: part if not all of what they earn will now have to go for medical expenses. All of these women are in danger of contracting venereal diseases and AIDS.

2. Defenselessness. They all try to "latch on" to a man (mar-

ried or not) who will provide them with a place to stay and a measure of protection.

3. Loss of dignity. A prostitute is dealt with by her partners as a mere object of gratification, and she rather readily submits to this demeaning attitude on their part.

4. Moral depravity. All of the subjects interviewed agreed that it is very rare for a man to treat them with any respect. They readily refer to certain men as "animals."

5. Weakness of will, and instability. These women are not sentimental. They simply walk off with the highest bidder. Some would like to give up their "profession," but in the words of one of their number: "It's like being sick. You have to take care of yourself."

6. Loss of femininity. The African woman is a wife and mother. It is by bringing children into the world that she wins respect. But in prostitution, motherhood is a misfortune. A child is regarded as an obstacle. Children of prostitutes are left to fend for themselves—locked up alone at night, growing untended like so many weeds, until they are old enough to join a gang or to begin working the streets with their mothers.

7. Abortion. Some prostitutes have recourse to induced abortion in order to maintain their freedom to practice their "profession" and not have to rear a family. The means they employ range from the application of pharmaceutical preparations, sometimes in lethal doses, to medicinal herbs that are often toxic, to obstetrical maneuvers at the hands of irresponsible health professionals, back-alley practitioners, or even the woman herself. Public opinion has a tendency to minimize the importance of the life destroyed by this act, as well as other consequences it frequently has. And yet, 80 percent of the cases of secondary sterility in consequence of an abortion, perforation of the uterus, intoxication with pharmaceutical products or medicinal herbs, local or general infections (chronic or acute), hemorrhage, shock, and sometimes death, are due to these maneuvers. The woman alone, then, is victimized by these procedures. It is she who must suffer all of the consequences.

What Can Be Done about Prostitution?

Most prostitutes come from large and often very poor families. Couples should be instructed in family planning and responsible parenthood. Broken homes and dysfunctional families place a disproportionate number of prostitutes on the streets. The evil of divorce must be combated, and couples should be helped to overcome their daily difficulties. It will be equally urgent to halt the practice of placing children with a number of different foster parents at the death of their father. Instead, the widow should be helped to meet the needs of her children by way of paid employment or an adequate small business.

Parents should see to it that their children are brought up with an appreciation of the value of personal effort, and endeavor to arouse in them a pride in the personal contributions they can make to the betterment of their race and all humanity. Boys and girls ought to share chores equally, so that children may learn self-respect from their earliest years.

Schools should offer adequate sexual instruction. Children should be able to obtain basic information in family education at school. It is of the utmost importance to offer seminars for youth on feminine and masculine psychology. And young people should be shown the dangers and risks of amorous adventures. Children should be taught that success in life costs effort. Girls must be dissuaded from attempting to corrupt their teachers by offering them either money or themselves. Our upbringing of our young people should encourage them to be guided by a life ideal, rather than by the pernicious influences of bad company.

True, prostitution is said to be the world's oldest profession. But the society can establish structures of respect and acceptance that will provide a chance for escape for those who really wish it. Here the battle for the liberation of African women should consist in a struggle against illiteracy, and an effort to help prostitutes recover the dignity that they must cast to the winds every time they step out of doors into the flood of jibes and ridicule awaiting them. Similarly, the social status of the widow merits the attention of all.

Generally speaking, one of the consequences of the institutionalization of corruption in our bureaucratic system is the prostitution of women. For example, take the primary school teacher who is passed over for promotion because she refuses her supervisor's advances. Obviously some of her colleagues must be more compliant! We must say that, generally speaking, women are subjected to a great deal of sexual harassment, in the workplace as elsewhere in their lives. This prompts us to pose the serious question of the nature of female-male relationships in Africa today.

In sum, we regard prostitution not only as the result of women's unsatisfactory living conditions today, but also as a cause of the degradation of all African society. After all, do we not have a saying: "Educate a woman, educate a nation"? In other words, the prostitution of women contaminates the soul of the population, and compromises the future of Africa.

The reality of sexuality clearly demonstrates that woman is not the weaker sex. She is rather the stronger sex. The difficulty here is that woman underrates and disclaims her strength. And it is this underestimation that impels her to reduce herself to the status of an object by becoming a prostitute. Prostitution challenges the conscience of all African women. Its basis lies in the organization of our society. It is the task of society, then, to provide a remedy. Its consequences affect not only the women who practice it, but all women, regardless of their social position.

Our church communities must take a more active role. In the pastoral letter on women published by Archbishop Kabanga of Lubumbashi, we read:

> The material poverty of our region, together with unemployment in our cities, are at the root of a great many ills in our humbler neighborhoods, like the inner cities of our large metropolitan centers. . . .
>
> We find, among other things, the prostitution of minor girls. Throughout our land, no philanthropic or Christian organization has taken responsibility for the rehabilitation of girls, sometimes older, sometimes quite young, who are caught in prostitution. The sight of these "London girls," as they are called, in the company of clients of every age, moves no one: not religious women, not mothers, not the civil authorities.[6]

In view of the problems cited by the prostitutes themselves, and with the present structures of modern education in Africa, we propose that the sexual and moral initiation of children and youths become the responsibility of our "Living Church Communities." Let the elders of the church (fathers and mothers) prepare the young (boys and girls) for married life.

SEXUALITY AND RELIGION

This part of my essay will be devoted essentially to a presentation of the viewpoint of the Roman Catholic Church on the question of sexuality. I shall cite certain official church documents, then examine the matter of the integration of the word of God into our culture.

What is at issue is the problem of inculturation in the matter of sexuality. The church is widely accused of burdening the faithful with an inordinate sense of guilt in this area. Yet the church seeks to be the guarantor of the covenant between God and the people of God — a covenant that can be observed only in the presence of a harmonious relationship between women and men created in the image of God.

Sexuality is in itself a worthy and good thing. It is part of God's own project. We read in Genesis 1:27 that the human being was created male and female in the image of God. Furthermore, in Genesis 1:26-28 the human couple is invited to subdue the earth and fill it, together, each according to his or her identity. Along the same lines, Genesis 2 and 3 present the complementary responsibilities of man and woman in God's plan for humanity.

Throughout salvation history, then, we observe a difference between man and woman, a difference reflecting both "nature" and "nurture." When God calls someone to a specific mission, God turns sometimes to woman, and other times to man. The vocation of women must be more honestly acknowledged and encouraged in African church communities. Women should feel that they are sharers in the construction of the Reign of God at the heart of the world.

The Teaching of the Church

The French bishops define sexuality in a new and very interesting way. They distinguish between the "genital" and the "sexual" component of the human makeup. They use the word "genital" to refer to "anything having to do with the sexual organs and the function of reproduction, as described by anatomy and physiology."

> Sexuality, on the other hand, refers to the feminine or masculine dimension marking the entire personality of every individual, from the first moment of his or her conception throughout the whole of that person's development. Accordingly, all human relationships are inevitably sexual. Any situation involving both men and women is experienced partly in function of their respective sexual identities, and in terms of the distinct role that each is called to perform.[7]

The same authors go on to say: "Contrary to what is still often thought, sexuality is not the sole affair of the more intimate aspects of one's personal life. It concerns all areas of social, economic, and political life. Conversely, it is also conditioned by them."[8]

The late Cardinal Malula regarded sexuality as a sacred matter. "It is not to be trifled with," he wrote. "The sexual power in human beings means that God wishes to associate men and women with the divine power of creation to bring into the world beings who are to live eternally. This is no casual matter." And His Eminence goes on to declare:

> If we observe closely, abstention from sexual relations before marriage, like the practice of the virtue of chastity generally, is nothing but obedience to the commandments of God, which are addressed to every human being. Youth should be frequently reminded of this. And experience shows that chastity constitutes a factor for expansion and great spiritual energy.[9]

As for the question of celibacy, we find the answer in Matthew 19:10-12 and 1 Corinthians 7. For the rest, let us simply say: "Remaining unmarried is not detrimental; on the contrary, it can be a source of growth."[10] Speaking to Christian families,

Pope John Paul II says: "God has created the human being in the divine image and likeness. In calling this being into existence *by* love, God has also called it *to* love."[11] The Holy Father further asserts:

> It is difficult to speak of sexuality today. Our times are marked by a disorientation which, while not difficult to understand, is unfortunately fomented in part by a veritable explosion of the sexual instinct. The union of bodies has always been the strongest language that two beings can address to each another. And therefore this language, which touches upon the sacred mystery of man and woman, prohibits one from ever performing the acts of love in the absence of the conditions of a total, definitive responsibility for one's partner, in a commitment that is made publicly, in marriage.[12]

Pope John Paul II, in his Apostolic Letter *On the Dignity and Calling of Woman*, states:

> Woman is the being in whom the order of love in the created world of persons finds a place to sink its first roots.
>
> The dignity of woman is measured in the order of love, which is essentially an order of justice and charity.
>
> Without recourse to this order and its primacy, no one can give a complete, adequate answer to the question of the dignity of woman and her calling. When we say that woman is "she who receives love in order to love in turn," we are not thinking solely or principally of the specific nuptial relationship of marriage. We are referring to something more universal—something founded on the very fact of being woman in the ensemble of interpersonal relationships that variously structure the coexistence and cooperation of all persons, men and women alike. In this broad, differentiated context, woman represents a particular value as a human person, and at the same time as a concrete person by virtue of the fact of her femaleness. This regards each and every woman, independently of the cultural context in which she finds herself, or her spiritual,

psychological, and physical characteristics, as for example her age, education, health, employment, or marital status.[13]

In light of the foregoing, we feel a profound gratitude to the dioceses and societies that have dared to assert themselves and help women acquire an awareness of their dignity. In the church as in the world, men and women are called to fulfill themselves not in opposition, not in rivalry, but together, with and facing each other, in marriage as in friendship or work.

On the matter of fidelity and the indissolubility of marriage, Vatican Council II declares:

It is a fundamental duty of the Church to assert and reassert, most emphatically, the teaching of the indissolubility of marriage in the hearing of those who, in our day, regard it as difficult, indeed impossible, to bind themselves to someone for life. To those, again, who have been reared in a culture which rejects the indissolubility of marriage and which condemns, even openly, a commitment on the part of spouses to fidelity, one must make once more the joyous proclamation of the definitive character of that conjugal love that finds in Jesus Christ its foundation and its strength.

Saint Matthew's gospel (19:1-11) is clear in the matter. "What God has joined together, let no one separate" (19:6).

It is difficult to summarize the position of the church on contraception. It is even more difficult to summarize the reactions to this position that come from other sources. One thing is certain: the matter of contraception is one of current importance for all marriages!

Father André Léonard writes:

The moral question of contraception arises from the fact that, with the human being, the structural bond between love and fertility is entrusted to the guardianship of freedom. In the animal world, reproduction occurs, one might say, mechanically, on the basis of the blind thrust of instinct. In the human species, however, the openness of a love between persons to the transmission of life, while writ large in the profound logic of sexuality, depends on the responsibility of the partners. Thus appears the notion of responsible fatherhood and motherhood.

Bringing a child into the world is of course not the result of an absolutely cold, rational decision or calculation. There is a legitimate element of improvisation and spontaneity in the sexual expression of love. But precisely for this reason, among others, the gift of life must not depend solely on the workings of instinctual desire or the laws of probability. Parents ought to transmit life, and determine the number of children that they will welcome into their home, with an eye to the genuine good of the couple themselves, the happiness of the child-to-be, the economic and social situation of the family, and the moral demands of openness to the gifts of God.[14]

But that leaves untouched the question of method. Here Father Léonard writes: "The stumbling block in the discussion ... consists in the church's distinction between artificial methods or contraceptives and natural methods, and its disapproval of the former.[15] We therefore urge the church to turn a more attentive ear to women, who, when all is said and done, are the ones most concerned in this question. We likewise urge the initiation of an intercultural dialogue in an area as delicate and intimate as the one we are considering.

On the subject of divorce and polygamy, Father Léonard writes:

The only conjugal bond that is in the image of Christ's love for his Church is the one intended to be exclusive—that is, monogamous, ... faithful, ... and irreversible, which means indissoluble. ... The first point—monogamy—has gradually become part of many cultures, and will continue to become part of them all. The gift of oneself, a gift at once spiritual and carnal, can be fully conferred, following the example of Jesus' own gift of himself to his spouse, only in exclusivity: "You and I till death."[16]

While modern society regards polygamy as an evil, in traditional societies it is looked upon as containing certain positive economic and social elements. This fact must not be ignored. For example, when a man is converted to the Christian faith, is it in the spirit of the gospel for him to repudiate wives to whom he has made a commitment, and destroy the family stability of his children? The church ought to address this question very carefully.

CONCLUSION

It is of primary importance that today's African woman undergo a change in mentality with regard to sexuality. To this purpose, society will have to divest itself of the negative component in its attitude toward female sexuality. Man and woman are partners. They both play the same role, in the sense that both share complete responsibility for their behavior. The African woman must therefore learn to define herself in terms of herself. She must learn to decide her life in all freedom. Accordingly, discriminatory practices will vanish only if she takes upon herself full responsibility for her education. Furthermore, her liberation will require a reconsideration of her social status. After all, we have come to see that her being is not defined exclusively in terms of her reproductive function.

Thus, the question of sexuality concerns everyone, men and women, in society as in our church communities. We must not, then, succumb to the temptation of simply excusing our weakness, however surely we may rely on the mercy of God. Rather let women think of their children, and of the world in which they would like those children to live tomorrow.

After an examination of the teachings of the church on sexuality, it is important to notice that the church includes both men and women. It is up to women, therefore, to reflect on their manner of life, both bodily and spiritual, in today's world. It will be very important to remind all persons of the need for a life ideal, and of the radicalism required by the gospel of those who would follow Jesus Christ.

Consecrated celibacy constitutes a capital value in the life of our Christian communities. It can help advance woman in her authentic calling as equal partner with man in all things, and not only where purely genital sexuality is concerned, by proclaiming the values of the Reign to come. It invites the world, and especially youth, to construct a kind of sibling relationship between man and woman, in which both will respect one another as children of the same parent. When all is said and done, what is needed in the area of sexuality is for God's word to become inculturated. After all, the gospel is a word of liberation for all of the peoples of the earth.

NOTES

1. See Kinyamba Shomba, *La sexualité préconjugale* (Kinshasa and Lubumbashi: Labossa, 1983), 21-52.

2. "Code de la Famille," *Journal Officiel de la République de Zaïre*, August 1987.

3. See B. Crine-Mavar, "Ethnies et langues," in *Les Atlas Jeune Afrique: République de Zaïre* (Paris: Jeune Afrique, 1978), 28.

4. Shomba, *Sexualité préconjugale*, 20-21.

5. Simone de Beauvoir, *Le deuxième sexe*, Idées (N.R.F., 1974).

6. Archbishop Kabanga, "Lettre Pastorale sur la femme," in *Dossiers Jeunes*, no. 17, ed. Mbegu (Lubumbashi: Saint Paul-Afrique, 1988).

7. In Commission Épiscopale Française de la Famille, *Sexualité et vie chrétienne* (Paris: Centurion, 1981), 17.

8. Ibid., 17-18.

9. Cardinal Malula, "Je m'engage à rester chaste," Pastoral Letter (Kinshasa, 1986), 5.

10. *Sexualité et vie chrétienne*, 81.

11. Pope John Paul II, "Les tâches de la famille chrétienne," *Discours du Pape et Chronique Romaine*, special no. 400 (December 1981), 25.

12. Idem, "Message aux jeunes de France," 1980.

13. Idem, *Sur la dignité et la vocation de la femme* (Kinshasa: Saint Paul-Afrique, 1988), 115-16.

14. André Léonard, *Jésus et ton corps: La morale sexuelle expliquée aux jeunes* (Lubumbashi: Saint Paul-Afrique, 1988), 37-38.

15. Ibid., 39.

16. Ibid., 31.

REFERENCES

Songue, Paulette. *Prostitution en Afrique: L'exemple de Yaoundé*. Paris: Harmattan, 1987.

Tshibanda wa Mwela Bujitu. *Femmes libres, femmes enchaînées.* Lubum-
bashi: Saint Paul-Afrique, 1978.
Tundu, Kialu. *Le Royaume de Bene-Kalundwe.* Memorandum for the
Licentiate in History. Lubumbashi: UNAZA, 1981.

PART 3

AFRICAN WOMEN
AND
THE CHRISTIAN CHURCH

11

Jesus Christ and the Liberation of Women in Africa

Teresa M. Hinga

In the emergent and emerging theologies of liberation, both in the West but particularly in the Third World, the question of christology has gained significant proportions. Theologians are trying to analyze and articulate the implications of Christianity and belief in Christ for their particular and often quite personal situations. A central question has been: Who is Christ? And what does belief in him mean, particularly for those who find themselves caught up in conditions of oppression?

This article attempts a reflection, however preliminary, on the implications of belief in Christ in the context of African women's search for liberation. It seeks to point out the ambivalence apparent in prevailing christologies, and the need for the evolution of an African feminist christology—or at least, the need to create pointers in the right direction.

In recognition of the fact that feminism in Africa is a relatively novel extension of feminism in the West, and also of the fact that Western feminist theologians have reflected to a considerable depth, though without seeming to reach an unequiv-

Teresa M. Hinga, a Kenyan, is Lecturer at Kenyatta University. She has a doctorate in Religious Studies from Lancaster University, England.

ocal consensus, on the relationship between christology and women, it is useful to reflect on what kind of ideas they have come up with so far.

A broad sweep of the Western feminist theologians' literature on the issue of christology reveals that there are at least two perspectives. On the one hand, there is what may be referred to as the radical feminist view, which is probably best epitomized in the works of Mary Daly. On the whole, this view holds that cultural and social institutions, including religion, are so irredeemably warped by patriarchy that they can hardly be considered as allies of women as they try to liberate themselves. On the contrary, patriarchal culture and other social institutions help to engender their oppression and subjugation. This goes both for religion and received theology articulated largely by people who are perceived to be sexist and "misogynist" in their approach.

Thinking specifically of christology, the doctrine of Christ, and the way it relates to women's liberation, Mary Daly, for example, advocates a rejection of the dogmas concerning Christ that have hitherto been formulated as largely oppressive of women. In her words:

> The distortion in Christian ideology resulting from and confirming sexual hierarchy is manifested not only in the doctrines of God and of the Fall but also in doctrines concerning Jesus. A great deal of Christian doctrine has been docetic, that is, it has not seriously accepted the fact that Jesus was a limited human being. A logical consequence of the liberation of women will be a loss of plausibility of Christological formulas which reflect and encourage idolatry in relation to the person of Jesus.[1]

Mary Daly is also highly critical of the way Jesus has been presented as a model of emulation for Christians, including women. Given the women's quest for liberation, Mary Daly suggests that imitating Christ as a model would only lead women to becoming more entrenched in the quagmire of subjugation. She argues that, insofar as received theology presents Christ as the primordial scapegoat, one who lives and dies entirely for another, his emulation would lead women to take on a role which they already are playing, for women, in any case, fulfill the role of victims and scapegoats in their various cultures. As she observes:

> The qualities that Christianity *idealizes*, especially for women, are also those of a victim: sacrificial love, passive acceptance of suffering, humility, meekness, etc. Since these are the qualities idealized in Jesus "who died for our sins," his functioning as a model reinforces the scapegoat syndrome for women. Given the victimized situation of the female in sexist society, these "virtues" are hardly the qualities that women should be encouraged to have. Moreover, since women cannot be "good" enough to measure up to this ideal, and since all are by sexual definition alien from the male savior, [Jesus] is an impossible model.[2]

Consequently, Mary Daly proposes that for women to succeed in their quest for liberation, they should learn not to look up to any models, least of all that of Jesus in his role as victim. In fact, Daly suggests that, for women to achieve their freedom, they will need to cultivate confidence in themselves, such that their actions spring from themselves, rather than being motivated by imitation of any role models.[3]

On the less extreme side of western feminist theological discourse lie the thoughts of those who, for want of better terminology, I would call "reformist." These represent the view that social institutions are not distorted beyond repair. It is felt that aspects of culture and religion are salvageable, and that theology can help women in their struggle for emancipation and justice. In this category fall feminist theologians like Rosemary Ruether, Elisabeth Moltmann, Phyllis Trible, and Elisabeth Schüssler Fiorenza, among others.

Rosemary Ruether well exemplifies our theme here, for she has reflected specifically on the implications of christology for women's liberation as she ponders on the question: Can a male savior save women?[4]

Ruether is mainly concerned with exposing the sexism embedded in some of the received christologies that have been handed down to society through the ages—a sexism that would be an obstacle in women's search for justice and liberation. Such sexism is, according to Ruether, manifest in some of the works of the great church theologians. In particular, she cites the works of Thomas Aquinas who presented the view that women are malformed males and therefore constitute the abnormal half of the human species. With his own peculiar logic, he went on to argue that this is the reason why the incarnation of God could only be in a male, Jesus. The "maleness" of Jesus is, therefore, for Aquinas, not incidental but arises out of (ontological) necessity. The male reflects through Jesus the fullness of the image of God. By the same logic, woman is naturally second-rate and, therefore, naturally subordinate to man. This kind of theologizing has led to a fixation on the "maleness" of Christ as a decisive factor in christology. It is a view often emphasized, for example, by those who oppose the ordination of women. The physical resemblance—that is, maleness[5]—is considered a necessary condition for those who represent Christ. Hence, priests are necessarily male!

However, as Ruether has rightly pointed out, the overfixation on the maleness of Jesus is a distortion of the truth as she sees it. For, indeed, it misses the whole point of the incarnation, namely, that Jesus became human in order to effect the redemption of humanity both male and female. In this way, Jesus represented God who, in Hebrew thought, was perceived as their liberator and their redeemer par excellence.

Despite the essential "misogynism" of the dominant christology in western theological thought, Ruether goes on to show that there did occasionally emerge in Western Christianity alternative though less pervasive christologies. Some of these she isolates and highlights as potentially useful for women, because they are more inclusive and less sexist.[6]

CHRISTOLOGY AND AFRICAN WOMEN:
THE AMBIVALENCE OF THE ENCOUNTER

In general, the above two perspectives reflect Western women's views concerning Jesus Christ and their specific context of a search for emancipation. At best, they reveal a certain ambivalence in their encounter with Christ. To which extent could these views be said to be universal? Could the same be said of the encounter between Christ and African women?

To be able to answer these questions, it is important to take into account the realization among contemporary theologians that Christ encounters people in various contexts. He has also been presented and appropriated in a variety of images or "faces" as Bonino prefers to call them. We have noted in this context that Ruether, for example, has isolated at least two such "faces" of Christ and has analyzed their implications for the women's cause. Another Latin American theologian[7] has discussed five images of Christ as appropriated by the Latin American masses, and their effects in engendering their oppression and powerlessness.

It would seem that in Africa, also, more than one image of Christ has been presented to and appropriated by Africans, including women, with, as I shall endeavor to show, mixed results.

Going back to history, we recall that during the period of colonial and imperial expansionism, the prevailing image of Christ was that of Christ the conqueror. Jesus was the warrior King, in whose name and banner (the cross) new territories, both physical and spiritual, would be fought for, annexed, and subjugated. An imperial Christianity thus had an imperial Christ to match. The Christ of the missionaries was a conquering Christ. Conversely, winning Africa for Christ was a major motivating factor in missionary zeal. Africa was the booty to be looted for Christ. What were the implications of this perception of Christ for the Africans?

The conquest of Africa often implied an erasing of most of what Africans held dear. The missionaries, in the name of Christ, sought to create a spiritual and cultural *tabula rasa* upon which they could inscribe a new culture, a new spirituality. This attempt at "erasing" was not all that successful, and, instead of creating a clean slate, the missionaries more often than not managed to create an identity crisis in the African minds—a sense of gross alienation. This is the kind of alienation and confusion that is lamented, for example, in Ngugi wa Thiongo's *The River*

Between, or Chinua Achebe's *Things Fall Apart.*[8]

The cultural and spiritual imperialism[9] of the missionary endeavor has had some dire consequences. In dealing with some of what they deemed to be obstacles in their battle for Africa on behalf of Christ, in their zeal the missionaries often did not pause to reflect adequately on the consequences for the persons they sought to convert. Many examples can be given here, but I will highlight only two.

In treating the issue of polygamy, for example, the missionaries acted in a manner that was largely detrimental to the welfare of the women concerned.[10] Often, the polygamist would be asked to abandon all but one of his wives as a condition for baptism. The policy of "disciplining" polygamists in this way undoubtedly brought untold pain to women and children thus discarded.

Another example which I give, because it comes from a culture I know well, is the issue of female circumcision encountered by missionaries in Kenya. Again, in their unilateral decision to stamp out what they considered to be a barbaric African custom, they ended up causing the women involved to suffer tremendously. Many a Protestant father was forced to sign, on pain of excommunication, that they would not circumcise their daughters. Meanwhile, their daughters continued to be exposed to a barrage of derision and ridicule for failing to undergo the rite that culturally defined them as women.[11] Many uncircumcised Protestant girls could not withstand the psychological torture, abuse and social ostracization that was poured upon them, and they were secretly circumcised anyway.

No doubt, however, many missionaries would not have agreed with the above interpretation of their actions. This is because at the overt and conscious level, they expressed the desire to liberate the Africans from what they perceived to be the clutches of the devil. They were ostensibly motivated by the zeal to save Africa from the evils of slave trade, and to redeem her people from the state of savagery and apparent godlessness. They thought that by so doing, they would be implementing the gospel of Christ the liberator—for they would be "proclaiming liberty to captives" and opening the prison for them that are bound.[12]

Thus, missionaries with a lot of commendable zeal were in

the forefront, for example, of the movement for the abolition of slave trade, the freeing of captured slaves, and their rehabilitation.[13]

When the missionaries ventured into the African interior, they established mission stations which often functioned as centers of refuge or, in the view of the missionaries, "centers of Christianity and civilization." It is illuminating in this context to note that at least initially, the people who were attracted to the mission were the socially disadvantaged. Thus, the White Fathers, for example, established their missions as orphanages, in which ransomed slave children could be taught self-reliance and "be brought up in the faith, away from the dangers of heathen environment."[14] In the same vein, another author observes that the people who were often attracted to the mission stations in Kikuyuland were from poor families. These people saw the mission community as a possible avenue for social and economic mobility and, for a time, sending children to school was an admission of poverty![15]

Moreover, the missionaries used education as a strategy for proselytization. This was welcomed by Africans as a means of social mobility, especially when education came to be correlated with a high economic status in the new secular sector.[16]

It was probably the perception of the emancipatory impulses within missionary Christianity, at this point, which led to the positive response given to Christianity by many Africans. We read in history books of mass conversions, and of the spectacular phenomenon in Uganda where within seven years of missionary work, there were African Christians ready to die for their new found faith.[17]

It is apparent that women also perceived these emancipatory impulses of the new religion and responded accordingly. Among the "refugees" who took shelter in mission stations were women, some of whom were trying to break away from unsatisfactory marriages or harsh parental control. Thus, it has been noted that a major component of the adherents to the AIM mission among the Kamba of Kenya were girls who revolted against parental control and fled to the missions.

It could be said, then, that these two images of Christ, that of Christ the conqueror who seemed to legitimize the subjugation of whole races, and Christ the liberator, glimpses of whom could sometimes be seen in some of the charity work that missionaries were doing for Africans, found expression in missionary praxis. The Christ of the missionary enterprise was, therefore, an ambivalent one. His encounter with Africans, including women, had ambiguous results, an ambiguity that many an African writer has not failed to notice and to highlight.

SOME ALTERNATIVE IMAGES OF CHRIST IN AFRICA AND THEIR IMPLICATIONS FOR WOMEN

While the above is a description of the christology that found expression in missionary praxis, it cannot be said to be coterminous with Christ as expressed through missionary teaching. In their presentation of Christian doctrine, for example, the missionaries often made reference to the Bible as the authoritative source of the doctrine.

Consequently, the Africans gained access to the various "images" of Christ enshrined in the New Testament. Through the Bible, Africans caught glimpses of who Christ was, and what loyalty to him implied for his followers. They appropriated one or several of these images of Christ and made them their own, despite the distortions apparent in missionary praxis. By way of illustration and conclusion, I will discuss here three quite "common" perceptions of Christ as understood by Africans, and their implications for women.

Firstly, there is the very popular conception of Jesus Christ as the personal savior and personal friend of those who believe in him. Quite contrary to the view that Christ demands their subjugation—whether politically, socially or culturally—many Africans have come to perceive that Jesus desires to accept them as they are, and to meet their needs at a very personal level. They have come to accept Jesus as the friend of the lonely and healer of those who are sick, whether spiritually or physically.

To some cynics, the view that Jesus is a personal friend, savior, or healer, smirks of an unwarranted "privatization" of the person of Jesus to fit a highly subjective context. To others, a confession of Christ as "personal" savior is an indication of

Pharisaism and gross pretentiousness on the side of those who make such claims. However, I would suggest that, while not ruling out the possibility of some Pharisaism, the image of Jesus as a personal friend has been one of the most popular among women, precisely because they need such a personal friend most. (Thus, the image of Christ who helps them to bear their griefs, loneliness and suffering is a welcome one indeed.)

Secondly, another also popular image of Christ is that which seems to blend christology with pneumatology. Jesus is seen as the embodiment of the Spirit, the power of God, and the dispenser of the same to those who follow him. This image of Christ is particularly popular in the so-called independent churches. In our search for a feminist christology, it may be pertinent to note that, by and large, the patrons of these movements are women, among other marginalized peoples. It is also noteworthy that, in these movements, where the power of the Spirit (of Christ) is accentuated, women are peculiarly articulate and much less inhibited and muted than in established churches. In this "pneumatic christology," then, Christ becomes the voice of the voiceless, the power of the powerless. Women, as victims of oppression and muteness in society, would, no doubt, find this image of Christ useful in their quest.

A third face of Christ, also derived from the New Testament, is the conception of Christ as an iconoclastic prophet. Jesus stands out in Scripture as a critic of the status quo, particularly when it engenders social injustices and marginalization of some in society. This is the kind of Christ whose "function" of "iconoclasm" is thought by many participants in the African independent churches to be "incarnated" in their founder members whom they sometimes hail as "Black Messiahs." These prophetic leaders in Africa have emerged in continuity with the prophetic role of Christ as the champion of the cause of the voiceless, and the vindicator of the marginalized in society.

In conclusion, I would suggest that in the African women's quest for a relevant christology, aspects of the above three images of Christ would form some of the defining characteristics of the Christ whom women confess.[18] For Christ to become meaningful in the context of women's search for emancipation, he would need to be a concrete and personal figure who engenders hope in the oppressed by taking their (women's) side, to give them confidence and courage to persevere.

Secondly, Christ would also need to be on the side of the powerless by giving them power and a voice to speak for themselves.[19]

Thirdly, the Christ whom women look for is one who is actively concerned with the lot of victims of social injustice and the dismantling of unjust social structures. Christ would, therefore, be expected to be on the side of women as they fight for the dismantling of sexism in society, a sexism that has oppressed them through the ages.

It goes without saying that, along with formulating a relevant christology, women would also need to be on the alert, and to be critical of any "versions" of christology that would be inimical to their cause. They would have to reject, like others before them, any christology that smirks of sexism, or that functions to entrench lopsided gender relations. Only in so doing would African women be able confidently to confess Christ as their liberator, as a partisan in their search for emancipation.

NOTES

1. Mary Daly, *Beyond God the Father* (Boston, Mass.: Beacon, Press, 1973), 69.

2. Ibid., 77.

3. Ibid., 67f. In this context, Daly seems to propose a spirituality for women that not only goes "beyond God the Father" but also beyond Christ. The sentiments of women who share Mary Daly's view have, therefore, been aptly described as post-Christian.

4. This is a question to which Ruether has addressed herself in her books *Sexism and God Talk* (Boston: Beacon, 1983, 116ff.), and *To Change the World* (New York: Crossroad, 1983, 45ff.).

5. As one feminist wit has observed, it is interesting to note that no one insists that priests also be Jews and thirty-three years old, to complete the physical resemblance with Jesus of Nazareth.

6. See Ruether, *Sexism,* 127–34. Here she isolates two traditions of christology, namely, androgynous christologies and spirit christologies.

7. See Dia Aranjo, in J. M. Bonino, *Faces of Jesus* (Maryknoll, New York: Orbis Books, 1984), 30–38.

8. See also Jean-Marc Éla, *African Cry* (Maryknoll, New York: Orbis Books, 1986), 9ff., and F. Ebousi-Boulaga, *Christianity without Fetishes* (Maryknoll, New York: Orbis Books, 1984).

9. This is, of course, not to mention that missionary Christianity seemed to provide the legitimating ideology for colonization and the exploitation of Africans that went with it. The alliance apparent between missionary religion and colonialism was not lost to Africans. Among the Agikuyu, for example, a telling adage was recounted, to the effect that there is no difference between the missionary priest and the colonial settler (*Gutiri muthungu na mubea*). An African lament reflects the same perception: "When the missionaries first came, they had the Bible and we had the land. Now they have the land and we have the Bible!"

10. This kind of tendency is still implicit in the ongoing debate about the merits or demerits of the institutions of polygamy in Africa. Many of the arguments are still given over women's heads; women are hardly consulted for their views.

11. For a detailed account of the upheaval that this particular problem occasioned in the relationship between missionaries and the Agikuyu, see Kamuyu wa Kang'ethe (1981). This work also records in detail the abusive song *Muthirigu*, which was purposely composed to wage psychological war on opponents of circumcision. The girls of Protestant families were particularly targeted in this song, and the psychological torture they underwent must have been tremendous.

12. Roland Oliver, *The Missionary Factor in East Africa* (Great Britain: Longman, 1966), 33.

13. Ibid., 31f.

14. Ibid., 47.

15. Strayer, Robert et al., *Protest Movements in Colonial East Africa* (Syracuse, New York: Syracuse University Press, 1973).

16. Strayer, Robert, *Inquiry into World Cultures — Kenya Focus on Nationalism* (New York: Prentice-Hall, 1973).

17. W. B. Anderson, *The Church in East Africa, 1840–1974* (Central Tanganyika Press, 1977), 23ff.

18. These three perceptions of Christ are discussed by way of illustration, and do not preclude the possibility of other "images" of Christ. These are discussed because of their prevalence and direct implications for the women's cause. It is the task of feminist theologians to analyze systematically further images of Christ prevailing in Africa to see whether they are "useful" or inimical to women's search for liberation. It would be interesting to analyze, for example, the relationship between mariology and christology and its implications for women in African Catholicism.

19. This view is directly derived from the gospel narratives of the life of Jesus, for they depict Jesus as a friend and a "pal" of the marginalized in his contemporary society. In his public ministry, Jesus is also depicted as a compassionate friend of the lonely and the suffering, whose liberation he undertakes.

12

Sexuality and Religion in a Matriarchal Society

Anne Nachisale Musopole

The subject of sexuality and religion has been discussed and written about by many people. Each one of them has written or spoken according to his or her understanding of the subject. I am going to share with you my understanding of women's sexuality and religion as a Malawian and a matriarchal woman. This essay will focus on how our matriarchal culture viewed sex in the context of indigenous religion. Then I will explain how Malawians, after being converted to Christianity, view woman's sexuality. Finally, I will raise questions based upon the conflict which was caused by this new religion and attempt to find a way to a true Christian faith in which both male and female would be human as God and Jesus intended them to be.

SEXUALITY AND INDIGENOUS RELIGION

Sexuality in this context is to be understood in terms of the difference between male and female gender, but the Chewa

Anne Nachisale Musopole of Malawi is involved in volunteer mission work, speaking in Presbyterian churches in the United States and leading Bible studies.

culture has not put much emphasis on the differences. The Chewa, a matriarchal culture in Central Malawi, believed and still believe that both male and female are children of God. In this society, women are viewed as a source of life and a medium of communication between God and humans. Women are viewed as a source of life, because both male and female children come from the woman's womb. The art of creating and sustaining life was understood as a secret between God and women. Women are builders of the community, because most of them are responsible for feeding the family. Most men never grow up even by the time they marry; they do not marry a wife, but a mother to take care of them.

In the villages, both men and women wake up early in the morning and go to the farm to till the ground. At daybreak both men and women come home, but the woman carries a bundle of firewood on her head. She carries two hoes in her hand and a baby at her back. The man just walks home with nothing in his hands. When they reach home, the man sits down to rest, while the woman makes fires and cooks food for the day. After eating, the man either sleeps or goes to drink beer at the nearby village. The woman never rests, but looks for food for the next day. The men do not give the women money to buy food. The woman is the primary source of nourishment and nurture.

Women are viewed as the medium of communication between God and humans because they were the ones who in traditional religion were prophets. The history of the beginning of women's ministry in the Chewa religion is lost in antiquity. Oral tradition has it that it began when chief Undi and his sister Mangadzi were on their way to the crowning ceremony. Mangadzi was caught up by the spirit of God, and she fell into a trance and spoke in tongues (*Kubwebweta*). After she calmed down, she interpreted what God had said to the people at the crowning ceremony. When the prophecy came to pass, Mangadzi was called *Makewana*, meaning mother of children. She was also called *Chauta*, meaning God's representative. Mangadzi had a revelation from God to build a shrine (*Kachisi*). She had assistants called *Matsano*, meaning representatives of the ancestor spirits. The duty of *Matsano* was to carry the elements for the sacrifices when the community was called out to worship God.

The women were responsible for the healing ministry, for praying for rain when there was drought in the land, and for leading the community in many other religious observances. The women were called rainmakers, hence, sustainers of life, for water is life.

WOMEN IN LEADERSHIP POSITIONS

From the thirteenth to the fifteenth centuries, the leadership of women was a common experience in many parts of Africa. My great-grandmother Anna Naphiri told me that African women were great militarists; on occasions, they led their men in battle. The Chewa culture produced a civilization in which men were secure enough to let women advance as far as their talent, royal lineage, and prerogatives would take them. Anna Naphiri said that her village suffered consistent attacks by Ngoni warriors. When the Ngoni ran away from the white man in South Africa, they dispersed into Central or East Africa. On their way, they killed people and stole their food and animals. During one of these attacks, her grandmother ordered men to hide underground. The women guarded the village, armed with spears, axes, and sticks. Some women were told to beat drums to announce the coming of the attackers. The Ngonis came with their war cries, and the women from my great-grandmother's side replied with their war cry, "Eh! Eh! Wanya!" meaning "Watch out, watch out, you are dead!" When the Ngonis saw women with spears jumping and striking the ground, they were surprised and they ran away. Men came out from hiding and pursued the Ngonis. Since that time, their village has not been attacked again.

I have also read about Asantehemaa Yaa Asantewa, a woman who led a plan for men in Asante to cut telephone wire and electrical lines in order to confront the British in what is now Ghana. Likewise, Queen Nzinga in Angola led the army of women to confront the Portuguese. There seems to have been more women in leadership positions before the attempted Westernization of Africa.

SEXUALITY AND CHRISTIAN RELIGION

 Christianity, as it was first brought to Africa, spells out that there is a dominant sex and a lesser sex. According to these teachings, man is dominant, and woman is the helper of man who must be obedient and submissive. The biblical myth of creation found in Genesis 2:18 points out that she is the helper. The Bible continues to say that woman stole the fruit which God had told them not to eat (Gen. 3:6–7), and since then woman has been called a sinner. Most preachers and all the missionaries who brought Christianity told Malawian men that women are sinners.

From 1983 to 1986, I was involved in a women's fellowship ministry with the Presbyterian church of Central Africa. I was a preacher in monthly meetings in the Lingadzi congregation and also led Bible studies in Area 15, which is a branch of the Lingadzi congregation. During Bible study periods we discussed women in the Bible at length. We found that God dealt with women in a divine-human communication which focused on acts of love and protection. God has led members of the women's community of faith and called them to positions of leadership. God gave the Holy Spirit to women then and has continued to do so even today.

We saw God as a liberator of women because we noted that even in the patriarchal community of Israel, God chose Deborah to lead and direct Israel. Deborah summoned Barak: Go and gather your men at Mount Tabor (Judges 4:6–7). In Susa, God chose Esther to liberate the Jews from death. Likewise, Esther gave a command: Go and gather all Jews to be found in Susa (Esther 4:16). Through these studies, we learned that even in the patriarchal tradition, when men were trembling, God chose strong women to stand up and fight for them.

When we studied the New Testament and learned that salvation, too, came into the world through a woman, we discovered from the Gospel of Luke that God became reconciled with human beings by sending an angel to Mary in a city of Galilee to say this:

> Hail, O favored one, the Lord is with you! Do not be afraid
> Mary, for you have found favor with God. And behold, you

will conceive in your womb and bear a son, and you shall call his name Jesus. (Luke 1:28, 30–31)

In this act, we saw God becoming reconciled with Malawian women, too, through Jesus, and we wondered why in our churches women are left out of important decisions, even those concerning women and children as members of the church. Should men not be made to realize that a man's God is born of a woman? When I compare Christianity to my culture, as a matriarchal person who believes in being included in decision making, I see Christianity is very oppressive to women.

The Presbyterian church of Central Africa, does not allow women to be ordained. When Jesus' message was preached to women in my country, many women experienced a new creation and felt the call to purchase a ticket to the express train of theology. But no sooner had they finished college and received their diplomas than they saw the women's wagon on the theological train toward church ministry slow down and grind to a sudden halt. These women, deprived of ordination, are found all over Malawian synods. These women did their training together with men in the theological college and did very well, but no ordination was permitted. Why? Because the tradition of the Presbyterian church claims to follow first-century Christianity in Europe, which does not allow women to be ordained. Malawi in the twentieth century adheres to this practice and may enter the twenty-first century doing the same.

As I continued to grow in my faith, I learned that Jesus of the New Testament was in touch with women throughout his ministry. The story begins two thousand years ago in the little town of Nazareth where Joseph and Mary lived. Joseph looked at the maiden Mary and wished her to be his wife. After he made his thoughts clear to Mary, she agreed to become his wife. Mary loved Joseph, and she awaited the day when they would be announced as husband and wife. While Mary was waiting for her wedding day and busying herself in preparing a wedding dress and other things which make a wedding wonderful, Yahweh of Israel looked down on earth and admired Mary and said in his heart: "This maiden is beautiful and lowly, I must make her a mother for my Son." God did not go into committee with anyone. God did not ask Joseph whether it was possible for the Divine to redeem humanity through Mary. In Mary God united divinity with humanity.

God has rewarded woman not according to her iniquities, as men of this world would have wanted. It must be shocking to our men to see that wonderful things come from and through woman who is deemed inferior. We see the righteousness of God with his redeeming mercy falling upon woman. God wanted to tell human beings not through a parable or a learned paper, but through a real event, that woman is human and a child of God. Women were elevated when one woman was chosen to be "the mother of the most high God." God's grace welcomes woman, makes her penitent, and redeems her. This is so surprising to me and the women in Malawi. We find it strange and incredible, in fact, to see men refuse to let women be near God, and continue to condemn them as sinners when God has already pardoned them. In a woman, I see a sinner who is seeking atonement and reconciliation with God. "Behold, I am the handmaid of the Lord" (Luke 1:38).

What I see in God's union with woman is the love of God that is the grace we have as women in our Lord Jesus. This act identifies Jesus with sinners although he knew no sin. God saw that sin will destroy people, and it is this knowledge that led God to send Jesus to save us all, women and men, and to bring us all into the household of God. Jesus comes for us all, not for men only. Human beings must learn not to disregard Jesus and denounce women. All men and women have sinned and fallen, and it is by grace alone that we are saved, whether men or women. God's pardon is for all who repent, whether men or women. This is what should guide the church's decisions and not the factor of gender and the implications of human sexuality.

POWER AND SEXUALITY

Why is it that the power relationship among God's children has traditionally been decided by gender? Hierarchy based on sexuality is wrong. In decision making and leadership in which the male is dominant, he accuses women who seek their freedom of attempting to be like men. The women are labelled "masculine," and this label has stuck because of the nature of its role-breaking powers. A woman who gets the label of "man" is one who breaks through male power socially, psychologically, economically, politically, or spiritually. People interpret women's desire for equality as masculine. This is so because for so long women have allowed themselves to depend on men. They have accepted being labelled weaker and tender vessels. To be feminine is to accept dependence on men.

Men are afraid to see their system of dominance being shaken by the advent of women who are practicing self-determination. They feel that as such women increase in number and fight for liberation, the long-established structure of sexual hierarchy may be forced with the times to crumble upon its foundations. Women's goal of liberation is not only to destroy men's dominance over them, but also to teach man the right way to be human. Liberation projects that have been launched by women in Africa are not aimed at domination of women over men. Women want to be free and successful, able to work hand in hand with men.

When Malawi got its independence from colonial rule, the President of Malawi, Dr. Kamuzu Banda, put much emphasis on the education of women. He encouraged women to aspire to higher education and higher positions in both the private sector and in the government. Women chiefs, village heads, and chairpersons for the party were appointed. Today, women are well represented in the House of Parliament and are working hand in hand with men. This is not so in the church. Although the Church of Scotland today has ordained women pastors, not so this church which is now independent and which grew out of its work in Malawi.

Women are working in a steady and organized fashion throughout the world, not to destroy but to reshape society. Women want to come out and claim a rightful place in society. For the women in Malawi, it is the men in the church who are oppressors. All people, men and women, must see and feel the change and be able to accept it.

In the patriarchal groups in Malawi, women are asking why the marriage arrangements of their daughters are being discussed and decided in their absence. Why should a daughter's affairs remain solely in the father's control? The church belittles women when it allows gatherings of women to be headed by men, as if women are not able to manage their own affairs. Because the church does this, it also condones patriarchal structures in society and is unable to adjudicate in cases of blatant sexism. This is illustrated by an incident in which the cattle which were the "payment" for the daughter of a Chitipa woman were received by the girl's father, who then used the payment without even asking permission of the girl's mother. It is sad that women should be treated like this.

This woman was a Christian friend, and we worshiped with her in a Mkono church. The husband, too, was a Christian until he received the cattle from his daughter's marriage. Such a double insult should not be tolerated by women. But it is an example of the indignities women are expected to accept. A woman is not allowed to make decisions in the house of a man. She has no right to things she produced or to the children to whom she gave birth. In the struggle for liberation, such women have not set out to hate men, but to prevent men from despising them. Women would be much happier to see men as friends, not as their tormentors or despisers. The right of women to defend their humanity must be seen as a right to defend what it means to live as truly human.

For this reason, women who feel this pain, who desire to be free from their oppression and who can no longer find partnership in unpredictable men, must march for their freedom. To these women, submission is, indeed, opposition to their struggle for independence. Enough is enough! They cannot be subordinate any longer, not even in bed, because it will no longer be pleasure, but pain. What can Paul say to these women? "Wives, be subject to your husbands, as to the Lord" (Eph. 5:22). No, Paul, not when these husbands do not show any signs of loving their wives as they do their own body. Submission to such men is submission to exploitation, which women now find difficult to accept.

The submission which God commanded in Genesis is twofold. "Man leaves his father and mother and cleaves to his wife and they become one." This is accepted in my culture, because before the Bible was introduced to us, men were already leaving their father and mother and coming to our village to beg for and cleave to women they love. In Genesis, the institution of marriage demands adjustment for both men and women. Women who cannot tolerate traditional male domination have a good reason to accept the call of Jesus: "Come to me all who labor and are heavy laden, and I will give you rest" (Matt. 11:28). Let them be revolutionaries for Jesus' sake. Let them be freed from the yoke of slavery in their homes, community, and church. Let them be free in the eyes of God.

Women from generation to generation have blindly accepted that men are of great value and that marriage means loving, even if the husband harasses them. They have accepted attack and aggression as being natural; they have believed that manliness means power, and womanliness means passivity and submission. This has been deeply implanted in the minds of old women who were brought up by the missionaries, but not in the minds of all women. This idea comes from authoritarian, patriarchal societies. My father-in-law, Rev. Y. R. Musopole, comes from this patriarchal culture, but his views on the above issue are quite different. He believes that women even in their culture must be given a fair chance to change, and he accepts the awakening social conscience and sense of justice for women in his culture. He looks at women with the eyes of Jesus and believes that all human beings are the children of God, and that women, too, must experience the freedom to worship and live happily in their homes not as objects, but as partners.

I have observed that the church implanted a feeling of dependence in women. Feelings of powerlessness and worthlessness make women unable to take hold of organizing their own lives. Therefore, they are forced to glorify their oppressors and allow them to dominate their minds. The oppressors look benevolent and powerful, but remember that Jesus said: The thief comes only to steal and kill and destroy; I have come that they may have life, and have it to the full. Men who dominate women are like thieves stealing the humanity of women.

DAUGHTERS OF AFRICA, ARISE! LUKE 8:40–42, 49–56

Like Jairus' daughter, we daughters of Africa have been dead, spiritually, of malnutrition caused by the injustice of the church.

Unlike Jairus, our fathers or brothers have not gone to ask Jesus to heal our sickness or snatch us from death. It is our mothers who have gone to Jesus to beg him to heal us. While our mothers are asking Jesus to heal us from the sickness of oppression, some of our brothers, uncles, and nephews have come to Jesus to say: "Your daughter is dead; do not trouble the teacher any more" (Luke 8:49).

However, Jesus has told our mothers not to fear, but only to believe, and their daughters shall be well. It is our fathers and brothers who are weeping and wailing to prevent Jesus from coming to our aid. They laugh and say, "Our daughters are dead; we do not need them in our church after all." But, Jesus comes to us and takes our hands and commands us to arise. Jesus has not only returned the spirit to us, but he has given the Holy Spirit to us to get up at once; he has directed us to live. Would that Africa be blessed with fathers like Jairus!

Meanwhile, as living persons, we have to do some work. We should do what many people did when they were healed by Jesus, which is to go to our families and tell them what the Lord has done for us, and how he has had mercy on us (Mark 5:19). Or we should do what another woman did when Jesus revealed to her what she did all her life: "Come, see a man who told me all that I ever did" (John 4:29).

On May 28, 1989, I was speaking with Margaret Nasoko from Malawi about the above topic. She asked: How can I arise and walk when our men continue to break my knee joints? How can I tell about Jesus when pastors instruct the young men about to be married to treat women as their helpers and not as partners? How can I arise when I am told that the day has not come for women in Malawi to work as pastors in the church of God? I chose to be a nurse because no man disturbs me in my job. Would that the church in Africa would demonstrate solidarity with women as Jairus did!

I am also asking you daughters of Africa: What is the most effective way of building an understanding of women's proper place in the church of Africa and of Malawi, in particular, in view of what we have discussed above? How can we make the church of Africa and of Malawi into a loving, understanding, loyal instrument of the Lord? How can we stop men from limiting and defining women's role to that of producing children, being good wives, and feeding the family? How can we help our sisters who are unmarried because they do not fit into the model the church has made? How do we help our sisters who are unable to produce babies to feel that they belong in the community of faith? How can we convince our old women who have believed that man is a god that he is not a god but human just like themselves? "Go and tell the brothers, I am ascending to my Father and your Father, to my God and your God" (John 20:17). What strategy should we use when the men refuse to allow us to tell what we know about Jesus?

Daughters of Africa, arise! Are we going to stand up and carry on the command of Jesus? What do we say?

13

The Priesthood of Church Women in the Nigerian Context

R. Modupe Owanikin

INTRODUCTION

The controversy over the issue of the ordination of women as priests in Christian churches has been going on for a long time. Seminars and workshops have been organized to discuss the issue, especially by the World Council of Churches. There has been a remarkable revolution against the conservative order of male chauvinism and domination practiced by the early mission churches on the part of women evangelists, visionaries, and church founders, mostly within the charismatic and Pentecostal folds in Nigeria. Already, a few women priests are found in Sweden, Switzerland, Canada, Kenya, Ghana, and Southern Africa, but not yet in Nigeria.

Despite these changes, the general phenomenon still reveals a resistance to change by churches of long origins and traditions, such as the Catholic, Anglican, Baptist, Methodist, and other churches. It would be an overstatement to declare the contro-

R. Modupe Owanikin, a Nigerian, lectures at Lagos University. She has a master's degree in New Testament Studies from the University of Ibadan, Nigeria.

versy resolved or to regard the low status of women in the church hierarchy as being permanently sealed. My task in this article is primarily to revisit the issue with a didactic approach and in the context of the traditions and culture of the Nigerian people.

Nigeria, like other parts of the world, is currently correcting the challenge of modernity that calls for modifications in some extraneous church doctrines in the quest to make Christianity relevant to modern Africa. The call for the ordination of women as priests in Nigerian churches can be said to fall within this framework.

The urgency of resolving the issue in question prompted the Lambeth Conference of Anglican bishops worldwide to include the issue on their agenda in London in 1988. Amongst other decisions, the Conference approved of the ordination of women as priests but under given conditions. Despite the acceptance of this resolution by the Nigerian Anglican archbishop, no woman priest has yet been ordained in the Anglican province of Nigeria. The same applies to other mission churches mentioned earlier. For our discussion to be coherent, some basic assumptions need to be defined here.

Various denominations of churches maintain diverse doctrinal and structural positions on the issue of women's ordination so much so that there is no uniform position and practice with regard to the priesthood of women that represents the view of the church in Nigeria in general.

Nigerian churches are of different denominations. There are the mission churches dating back centuries and imported into Nigeria from overseas. These include the Catholic, Anglican, Baptist, Methodist and Sudan Interior Mission, among many others. These generally do not have women priests. There are the Nigerian indigenous churches that are Pentecostal in nature, but that originated partly as a reaction against European imperialism in the mission churches and partly from genuine spiritual experiences. Typical of this category are the Aladura (Praying Churches), whose emphasis is on the spontaneity and simplicity of the divine spiritual call and on charismatic gifts. These churches are often founded by women and have numerous leading prophetesses. Then we have the new breed of "Gospel Evangelicals," so called because of their claim to preaching the full gospel message accompanied by a practical demonstration of charismatic gifts. The effect of the differences in church denominations and in their doctrines is the fact that the non-ordination of women is not a problem common to all the churches, but one experienced by only some, and chiefly by the orthodox mission churches such as the Anglican, Catholic and Baptists. Perhaps the long traditions of these churches, which are characterized by rigid conservatism, contribute to this attitude. The problem of non-ordination of women is not found among the Pentecostal churches.

Ordination can be defined as the act or ceremony of making someone a religious leader or priest.[1] It goes beyond mere appointment or self-appointment; rather, in the Christian context, it involves training as ordinands and a religious ceremony in which the candidate for ordination swears an oath and is consecrated before a congregation. This entitles the ordained person to serve henceforth as a priest with the privilege of administering the sacraments, such as the Eucharist. Titles such as Reverend, Evangelist, and, in the Pentecostal churches, Apostles, Prophets, and so forth, are taken by ordained priests. Not all church leaders are priests. The priest can be defined as "a person, especially a man, specially trained for various religious duties (such as, performing certain holy ceremonies and services) and for helping other people."[2] Thus, on a large scale, the term "priest" covers dedicated and ordained church ministers, but it must be noted that not all church functionaries can be regarded as priests. For example, prophets and prophetesses in Pentecostal or charismatic churches may be so called because of their prophetic gifts, independent of their training and ordination. Thus, in my treatment of the priesthood of women, I refer to women not just as church founders and leaders, but more to their involvement in priestly service in a wider context, particularly in the conventional mission churches.

Before proceeding to the relevant arguments, it is imperative that we briefly take note of the Nigerian context in which we are considering the ordination of women. Traditional Nigerian societies can be rightly described as male chauvinist. Women are regarded as playing second fiddle in all areas of life.

In several cases, women or wives are considered the property of the man. Perhaps the male-dominated occupational and social role structure in times past contributed to the pro-male prejudice. In this light, women, though made chiefs in communities, were never regarded as being equal with men and thus hardly occupied rulership positions. Though the traditional religion of the people recognized women as priestesses, this is more often than not due to the peculiar characteristics of the deities themselves. For example, Osun of Osogbo is a goddess, and it makes sense for her to be venerated mostly by women under the ministration of a priestess. The main thrust here is to show that the later Christian prejudice concerning the status of women in the church could be rooted in the Nigerian people's culture and tradition. It is noteworthy that the current women's liberation movement under the auspices of the Nigerian Council of Women Societies and the Nigerian Army Officers' Wives Association are gradually challenging and reversing the subordinate status of women in Nigeria.

THE DEBATE

Anti-ordination

Just as there are arguments in support of as well as against any idea, so there are proponents and opponents on the issue of ordination of women. This is tied up with the fact that attitudes towards women are always tinged with a certain cultural bias.

In India, for example, a woman is believed to be unworthy of salvation until she dies and reincarnates as a man.[3] In fact, to be born a woman is the result of bad karma. Until recently, Africa, like other parts of the world, had an inferior concept of women. In Africa, the birth of a son is greeted with joy and songs while a baby girl in some cases is greeted with silence and disappointment, especially if the parents do not yet have a son. The result is that the baby girl is less cared for and is more likely to be malnourished and brain damaged[4] in case of famine or other calamities.

The common argument against women playing a leadership role in the church is that women are divinely decreed to be subordinate to men, and thus there was no basis for their ruling over men in whatever capacity. Paul's injunction in 1 Timothy 2:11–12 that women should not speak publicly in church is often cited in support of this discriminatory position. Some argue that God is conceived of as male, though this is only anthropomorphic. Jesus and his twelve apostles were also males. All priests in Judaism were male.

The subjective role of wives to their husbands as taught in the Bible is sometimes taken to indicate their subordinate roles in the larger community. Perhaps the lowly status of women in Jewish society was carried over to the early Christian idea of women's roles in religious ceremonies and assemblies. The conservatives tenaciously reject the possibility of women priests and resist calls for radical revolution of this practice. However, the situation has been aptly helped by the growing incidents of independent Pentecostal churches and ministries in which women have demonstrated remarkable leadership and priestly gifts. This notwithstanding, mission churches still maintain the long-established tradition of the male monopoly on priesthood.

Women are sometimes portrayed as the weaker vessel. The fall of humanity at Eden through Eve is regarded as evidence of female vulnerability.

Walter Trobisch, in his interesting book on love, pictures women in the following Indian creation myth.

When he had finished creating the man, the creator realized that he had used up all the concrete elements. There was nothing solid, nothing compact or hard, left over to create the woman. After thinking for a long time, the creator took the roundness of the moon, the flexibility of a clinging vine and the trembling of grass, the slenderness of a seed and the blossoming of flowers, the lightness of leaves and the serenity of the sunshine, the fears of clouds and the instability of the wind, the fearfulness of a rabbit and the vanity of a peacock, the softness of a bird's breast and the hardness of a diamond, the sweetness of honey and the cruelty of a tiger, the burning of fire and the coldness of snow, the talkativeness of a magpie and the singing of a nightingale, the falseness of a crane and the faithfulness of a mother lion. Mixing all these non-solid elements together, the creator created the woman and gave her to the man.[5]

It is noteworthy that the above concept, though emotionally descriptive of feminine inclinations and tendencies, reveals a prejudiced anti-feminine and pro-masculine stance that sees nothing good in woman that is concrete and progressive. The Nigerian women's growing involvement in occupations formerly the exclusive reserve of males is evidence of a gradual reversal of the lowly status of women.

Women are sometimes seen as ritually unclean. The church is a holy place, as are the sacraments administered there. Officiation at worship and church administration are usually the exclusive prerogative of holy people. The flow of blood during menstruation as well as during childbirth are regarded as unclean. In some churches, particularly the Aladura Pentecostal or the Celestial Church of Christ, women who have just experienced these are usually required to undergo purification rites to ensure their fitness to worship in church. In some cases, chairs sat upon by women are not used by men. On the basis of the above, opponents of women's ordination advance the argument that because they are occasionally unclean, women (when compared to men who always maintain a constant biological state) cannot be qualified to serve as priests. The usual long period of pregnancy is further seen as a possible impediment and distraction for women priests.

Even though women may be celibate (as in the Roman Catholic church) they still do not rise up in the church's hierarchy as priests. In some Aladura churches, even those founded by women, women are not allowed to say the Benediction.

Pro-ordination

The exclusion of women from priesthood is not directly supported by Scripture. Jesus did not rule out women from the priestly vocation. In fact, Jesus preached equality of men and women. Though his twelve apostles were males, the role of women and the place Jesus gave them in his ministry cannot be underestimated. Mary, the mother of Jesus, Mary Magdalene (who first saw the risen Jesus), and Martha stand out as religious exemplars. In the early church, Priscilla and Phoebe occupied important positions, as will be examined later.

The concept of God as masculine has been questioned. On one hand, the use of masculine pronouns (he, him) for God could be for convenience. There is a sense in which God could be androgynous (that is both male and female). African traditional religion, for example, has in its pantheon some androgynous divinities, such as Nana Buluku among the Ewe and Fon peoples.[6] The Christian concept of a male God is based on the Old Testament account in Genesis of Yahweh's utterance, "Let us make humankind in our own image . . . In the image of God he created them; male and female he created them" (Gen. 1:26–27).

Man was created before woman and so, logically, God would be male since Adam was the first to be created by God in God's own image. Nevertheless, the phrase "male and female he created them" is still problematic since both man and woman bear the likeness and image of God. Most Christians do not conceive of God in androgynous terms; yet even Jesus' claim of possessing similar form as God (John 14:7) does not support the argument of an exclusively male God. The issue is open, and those in favor of women's ordination believe that there is no strong basis for using God's supposed male gender as argument for female inferiority. Moreover, the biblical phrase "God is spirit" postulates the unphysical nature and the neutral gender of God.

The priestly vocation is usually the result of God's call. People who receive the divine call of God respond by undertaking training to serve as priests. The importance of the call is that it is God who takes the initiative of choosing persons for the priesthood; the initiative is not dependent on human discretion. Inasmuch as females have not been excluded from the call of God, women who are called can, therefore, be seen to qualify for priesthood in fulfillment of God's call. For men to exclude women who believe they are called by God to the priestly ministry would amount to limiting God and replacing God's will with human will and prejudices with all their errors and inconsistencies. On this basis, the ordination of women to the priest-hood should be taken for granted.

It has been argued that male egocentricity lies at the root of the subordination of women. Though women may be physically the weaker sex, this is no reason to exclude them from the priest-hood, which does not require any sort of exercise of brute force. Neither is emotional instability the exclusive province of women. Concerning ritual uncleanness, it is apparent that this view of women's menstrual flow and childbirth derives from Jewish tra-dition. Then, too, the period of women's menstruation is limited and thus hardly inhibits their functioning as priests. Moreover, men also suffer from impurities of other kinds, and therefore the charge of impurities ought to apply to both genders. It must be noted that despite the above arguments against women, women the world over have occupied various leadership posi-tions as heads of governments (in Britain, Israel, India, the Phil-ippines, and Pakistan), as business magnates, and as vice-chancellors of universities, such as Benin and Lagos State Uni-versities in Nigeria. In fact, some evangelical churches such as the Foursquare Gospel church and the Apostolic Faith in Nige-ria were founded by women. All these examples show that women are suited to the priesthood and to prevent this is an anomaly.

THE BIBLICAL POSITION

Some scriptural material has been interpreted to support or to oppose the status and role of women in society as well as in the church. We shall briefly examine some of them. In Genesis 2:18 God said, "It is not good that the man should be alone. I will make him a helper fit for him." The creation of the woman sprang from God's wise and fatherly solicitude for man. Man needed *ezer kenegdo* (a helper corresponding to him). The trans-lation "helpmate" does not do justice to the full meaning of the phrase *ezer kenegdo*, which implies the notion of similarity as well as supplementation. The *ezer* has to be like him and at the same time not identical with him. She will be his counterpart and his complement. According to Delitzsch, woman is to man as the mirror of himself in which he recognizes himself.[7] Although this interpretation is often used as a basis for women's servitude to men, it could equally be regarded as indicating the inevitability of the union of both man and woman in which both share equal importance.

St. Paul is undoubtedly the biblical writer most accused of antifeminism. His writings reveal this:

> The woman should keep silent in the churches. For they are not permitted to speak, but should be subordinate, even as the law says. If there is anything they desire to know, let them ask their husbands at home. For it is shameful for a woman to speak in the church. (1 Cor. 14:34–35)

There is some degree of doubt about the place of this passage in Scripture. It is found at the above location, for example, in the Chester Beatty Papyrus as well as in the Codices Sinaiticus and Alexandrinus. But the passage is put after 1 Corinthians 14:40 in the Bezae Cantabrigensis and Ambroister.[8] In this context, Paul's injunctions emphasized 14:40, which warns that "all things should be done decently and in order." The danger here is that this dislocation could cast some doubt on the Pauline authorship of the passage. However, this would be unlikely when we examine the following teaching by Paul:

> Let a woman learn in silence with all submissiveness. I permit no woman to teach or to have authority over men; she is to keep silent. For Adam was formed first, then Eve; and Adam was not deceived but the woman was deceived and became a transgressor. (1 Tim. 2:11–14)

The uncompromising declarations by Paul are further compounded by the solemn attribution of his position on the women's question to God's will. He says, "If any man thinks himself to be a prophet, or spiritual, let him acknowledge that the things that I write unto you are the commandments of the Lord. But if any man be ignorant let him be ignorant" (1 Cor. 14:37–38).

As Kenneth Hagin rightly observes that Paul's injunctions contradict the practice in Pentecostal churches today:

> The passage commanding women to keep silent in the churches is in chapter 14 of 1 Corinthians—the great Pentecostal chapter. And whoever saw a Pentecostal church where the women kept silent and were not permitted to speak?
>
> In no other churches I know of are women more free to speak, teach, pray, shout and hold responsible positions than in Pentecostal or full Gospel assemblies. Yet no louder claim is made to follow the word of God wholly and solely than the claim of full Gospel and Pentecostal churches. In fact, that's what is meant by full Gospel following the full truth. And in full Gospel and Pentecostal Bible schools and seminaries women and girls are found studying the word of God in preparation for distinctively Christian service as missionaries, evangelists and preachers.[9]

It is likely that the above tendency in nonorthodox mission churches is due to their liberal interpretation of Scripture combined with the growing emphasis on spontaneous manifestation of the charismata (gifts of the Holy Spirit). For the orthodox churches not to follow this wave gives them the label of conservatives. Perhaps this accounts for the different positions on the priesthood of women in the church.

It is significant to note that Paul's stance on women's role in the church is not essentially antifeminist but rather arises from his recognition of the women church leaders of his time. In Romans 16:1, Paul wrote, "I commend to you our sister Phoebe, a deaconess of the church at Cenchreae." And in Romans 16:3 Paul went on to "greet Priscilla and Aquila [Priscilla's husband], my fellow workers in Christ Jesus." Tryphaena and Tryphosa, too, are women whom Paul commends as workers in the Lord (Romans 16:12).

The dual position of Paul raises problems of contradiction which have yet to be resolved among scholars. However, Paul's injunction on women could be due to his Jewish background and his love for respect and orderliness in the church, while, at the same time, he does not exclude gifted and pious women from general Christian service. Paul's view of women's role in worship could thus be left to the discretion of interpreters of his message. In general, he affirms the equality of all people under God and in Christ:

> For in Christ Jesus, you are all children of God through faith. For as many of you as were baptized unto Christ have put on Christ. There is neither slave nor free, there is neither male nor female, for you are all one in Christ Jesus. (Gal. 3:26-28)

According to Miriam Neff, "Our position before God as Christian men and women is equal; our experiences in life are not. We are equal (1) because we were both made by Him (1 John 3:1ff., Prov. 22:2, Gen. 1:27 and (2) because we were both redeemed by Christ and made by Him (Rev. 5:9, Eph. 4:4)."[10]

Yet, though man and woman are equal, their role in spiritual matters cannot be said to be so. As Charles Ryrie rightly observed:

> There can be no doubt that Jesus considered the two sexes equal. However, as regards spiritual activity, there was a difference between that of men and women. It is significant that Jesus chose and sent out seventy men. It is significant that there was no woman chosen among the twelve disciples.[11]

All the above show that men and women can, indeed, be taken as equals before God, but that their roles in the church differ. But to what extent women's roles of service in the church are limited has yet to be decided, and that includes the question of ordained ministry.

CHRISTIAN WOMEN IN NIGERIA

Traditional Nigerian society values women as partners to men in reproduction, maintenance of the homestead, economic sustenance, and moral education of the younger generation. Women as wives and mothers are respected and cared for by their husbands and later in life by their children. Numerous songs portray mothers as invaluable assets in the progress and well-being of society.

Women in Nigeria are not considered equal to men. In particular, their physical nature, weak in comparison to men, puts them in a secondary position in the largely agrarian Nigerian communities. The husband is unquestionably the head of his wife. In the olden times, as in old India, a Nigerian woman could be buried along with her dead spouse to continue to serve him in the next life.

In traditional religion, the deities in the pantheon include females such as Yemoja, Olokun, Oshun, and so forth. These have their numerous votaries and wield tremendous influence in communities near rivers such as Oshogbo in Western Nigeria. It is of interest, therefore, that traditional Nigerian religion recognizes the priesthood of women. Priests and priestesses abound and have equal status and authority in the religion. Women are not discriminated against but are even revered as mothers of society and exemplars in dedicated and resolute defense of their people, as in the story of Moremi and her son, Oluorogbo.[12]

Women are not totally disqualified from leading traditional worship because of so-called ritual uncleanness. Though menstruating women must afterwards undergo purification before offering worship and sacrifice in the temple or shrine, they continue their priestly role to men, and their contributions to the progress and political well-being of their respective peoples are acknowledged even up to the present day.

Our major thrust here is to show that Nigerian custom and traditional religion recognize the priesthood of women, and that this could be used as a model in the inculturation of Christianity in Africa. "Africa has also shaped to its own life the Christian message brought to it. It is widely acknowledged that the independent churches grew up all over Africa in response to the desire for a church where Africans may feel at home. This desire also shaped the worship, beliefs and practices of the traditional churches to make these churches distinctly African."[13]

It is in the light of the above that women have been allowed to enjoy a higher status and privileges in the Nigerian independent Pentecostal churches. These are perhaps largely influenced by the status of women in traditional religion. It is no wonder, therefore, that numerous prophetesses and female church founders abound in the Aladura. For instance, we have Captain (Mrs.) Emmanuel Abiodun, the cofounder and present head of the Cherubim and Seraphim church.[14] Other women include Lady Evangelist Bola Are of Agbala Daniel church in Ibadan, and Lady Evangelist Bola Odeleka of Agbara Olorun Kiibati (God's power is supreme) ministry in Lagos.

CONCLUSION

The role of women in the development of Christianity in Nigeria cannot be underestimated. The discrimination against the priesthood of women in some Nigerian churches, particularly the mission churches, is a carryover mentality which must be updated. Though the physical superiority of males over females is supported in Scripture, the female worthiness to serve as priests is not repudiated. Advocates of women's liberation are gradually viewing religion as an oppressor of women, although it must be accepted that the ultimate objectives of some modern-day women's organizations are too radical for some Christian believers. Theological reasons often cited for the exclusion of women from the priesthood may be an attempt to justify the status quo by resting on a mistaken interpretation of the New Testament message.

The increasing call for modernization[15] of conservative mission churches by its younger members, the increasing number of female church founders, the prominent role of women in indigenous churches, and the increasing worldwide clamor for women priests as manifested in the Anglican Lambeth Conference of 1988 are solid reasons for the ordination of women in the church throughout the world. In this way, the role of the church as an agent of social and moral change can be better appreciated. The priesthood of Christian women in Nigeria would be a further achievement in the struggle to acculturate Christianity in Nigeria.

NOTES

1. Paul Procter, ed., *Longman Dictionary of Contemporary English* (London: Longman, 1978), 766.

2. Ibid., 867.

3. D. L. Carmody, *Women and World Religions* (Nashville, TN: Abingdon, 1975), 45.

4. "Women in Crisis," World Vision & International Telethon (September 1982).

5. Walter Trobisch, *Love Is a Feeling To Be Learned* (Downer's Grove, IL: InterVarsity Press, 1968), 7f.

6. J. O. Awolalu and P. A. Dopamu, *West African Traditional Religion* (Ibadan: Oninbonoje, 1979).

7. F. Delitzsch, *A New Commentary on Genesis* (Grand Rapids, Michigan: Kregel, 1988).

8. K. Aland et al., eds., *The Greek New Testament* (London: United Bible Societies, 1975), 611.

9. K. E. Hagin, *The Woman Question* (Oklahoma: Faith Library Publications, 1979), 124.

10. Miriam Neff, *Discover Your Worth* (Wheaton, IL: Victor Books, 1979), 165.

11. Charles Ryrie, *The Role of Woman in the Church* (Chicago: Moody Press, 1958), 28–29.

12. E. B. Idowu, *Olodumare: God in Yoruba Belief* (New York: Praeger; London: Longman, 1962), 204-205.

13. Calvin Rieber, "Christianity as an African Religion," in W.S. Booth, Jr., ed., *African Religion* (Lagos: NOK, 1979), 269.

14. Akin Omoyajowo, *Cherubim and Seraphim, The History of an African Independent Church* (Lagos: NOK), 8.

15. Charismatic groups in Roman Catholic and Anglican churches, for example, are now radically changing or challenging the mission churches' position on the workings of spiritual gifts in the church in modern times.

The Will To Arise:
Reflections on Luke 8:40–56

Teresa Okure

This passage presents Jesus interacting with a number of characters: the crowds, Jairus concerned about his dying daughter, the woman with the flow of blood, Peter and the disciples, the messenger who comes to announce the death of Jairus' daughter, the mourning crowd, the father and mother of the dead child, and the child raised to life. The scene is preceded by the episode of the Gerasene demoniac (Luke 8:26–39). It continues with Jesus sending the Twelve to preach the Good News and to heal (Luke 9:1–6). In this reflection, we seek to savor the story in itself and to draw meaning for ourselves from the interactions between Jesus and these characters.

Jesus has just returned from the country of the Gerasenes where he cured a demoniac and was as a result urged by the inhabitants to leave their country. His own people had been waiting for him and were happy to see him back, they welcomed him. The scene presents a reception different from that in Luke

Teresa Okure, a Nigerian, is Dean of Studies at the Catholic Institute of West Africa in Port Harcourt, Nigeria, and Executive Secretary of the Ecumenical Association of Third World Theologians (EATWOT). A religious sister, she has a doctorate in New Testament Studies from Fordham University, New York.

4:24 (cf. John 4:44), where Jesus declares that a prophet finds honor *except* in his own home. The unexpected has happened.

Jesus is welcomed by the waiting crowd. The crowd is a nameless, faceless group. Their interaction with him is quite impersonal. In the midst of this impersonal encounter emerges Jairus, a father, an individual with a concrete, urgent need. He is a key person in the community, a ruler of the synagogue—in the African context, a village chief. He has just one daughter; she is not only ill but dying. The situation is desperate for the father. He needs Jesus' help most urgently. The urgency of his need is registered by his prostrate posture before Jesus. He comes to him openly, falls at his feet, and pleads with him to come and cure his dying daughter. Jesus responds to his request immediately and sets out with him on the healing journey.

En route, we encounter the crowd milling around Jesus once more. Then comes another human being in dire need, a woman who has suffered from an issue of blood for twelve years. She had tried all avenues of cure but nobody could cure her. Her situation is thus as desperate as that of the dying daughter of Jairus: two women, or rather a young girl and a woman in dire need of personal help, personal in the sense that their needs concern their own persons, their very lives and bodies. Unlike Jairus, the woman with the flow of blood does not approach Jesus openly; the traditions of society made that impossible. A woman with a flow of blood was a source of uncleanliness and contamination (Lev. 15:25–30); if she touched Jesus, she would make him unclean. Another possible reason for the approach from behind is that in Jewish society it was considered indecent for a woman to speak publicly with a man, let alone touch him. So the woman's action in approaching Jesus from behind is dictated by the sociocultural norms of her society. But the one thing which these practices did not succeed in doing was to deter the woman from her determination to be healed and thus from finding her own way to Jesus. This is an important point in the story, and we shall come back to it.

The woman steals up from behind and touches, not a part of Jesus' body—she has no intention of defiling him—but just the hem of his garment. She is persuaded that the least physical contact with him, even if it is indirectly through his garment, will convey healing power from him to her (cf. Mark 5:28). If we recall the importance that not only Africans but peoples of all religions attach to relics, we will understand the power behind the woman's reasoning. She believed that she could get the cure that she desperately needed without openly breaking the sociocultural practices of her people. We note that defilement extended beyond bodily touch. Anything that touched an unclean person possessed a contaminating power (cf. Lev. 15:26–27). Conversely, anything that touched a holy person also possessed a sanctifying power. The woman touched Jesus' garment and became cured. Power went out of Jesus and healed her. She knew in herself that she was cured.

Then Jesus in turn confessed that something had happened to him; someone had touched him. All around denied doing it, and Peter tried to tell Jesus that there was nothing extraordinary about his being touched by somebody, given the pressure of the crowd. But the woman's touch was not just an impersonal, unintentional, crowd-conditioned touch. It was a deliberate, meaningful, prayerful, personal touch. Only Jesus and the woman knew this. The woman touched Jesus, and Jesus responded to the touch; he allowed himself to be touched in the core of his being. The depth of the woman's faith and desire for healing was touching his depth. They met in spirit; they also needed to meet in person, openly. The woman had to be brought to this level of encounter. Hence, when she realized that there was no way of hiding what she had done, she came forward trembling (when Jairus came forward he was not trembling; unlike the woman, he did not have to fear the possible scorn of the crowd for doing something forbidden) and confessed what she had done. Jesus did not bring her forward in order to disgrace her or condemn her for touching him, but in order to set her mind at peace, make known her deep faith, assure her that her faith had effected the cure, assure her that she did well, that she had not defiled him. We do not defile God when we touch him; rather, we are sanctified by God.

Jesus praised the woman for her faith and told her to go in peace. Peace has to do with being and feeling at home in one's own self, with one's own neighbors, in one's society, free from all fears. Peace has to do with fullness of life, with physical, emotional, mental, and spiritual well-being. It has to do with knowing that someone understands us and cares for us. All this the woman found in Jesus when he said to her, "Go in peace." Jesus called her "daughter" and he established an endearing relationship with her. Before that she was just a woman with a flow of blood.

The story then continues with Jesus' healing journey to the daughter of Jairus. This time, another nameless figure appears — the messenger who comes to announce that the daughter is dead, thanks perhaps to the woman with the flow of blood for delaying Jesus on the way! He tells the father of the girl not to trouble Jesus any further. This is just common sense. But Jesus intervenes; all that the father has to do is believe. He continues the journey with the girl's father, and on arrival meets the professional mourners. He tells them to stop mourning, because the child is sleeping, not dead, and his remark only succeeds in making him a laughingstock before the people. Unperturbed, Jesus takes the father and mother of the girl, Peter, James, and John, goes into the girl's room and simply tells her, "Child, arise." The child gets up on her own and Jesus asks them to give her something to eat.

Eating in the New Testament, specifically in the Lucan tradition, seems to have been a proof that somebody was really physically alive. Jesus himself asked for something to eat to prove to his disciples that he had really risen from the dead (Luke 24:41–43); Lazarus, after being raised from the dead, had a party thrown in Jesus' honor (John 12:2). Food keeps each one of us alive with our own life, not with somebody else's life. The daughter of Jairus was raised to life; she was to continue living her own life if she was to be of any comfort to her parents. She had to be personally alive before she could be of any comfort to her parents. On the other hand, her life would be lacking if she failed to be a comfort to her parents. The parents of the girl were beside themselves with wonder at what Jesus had done. But for Jesus himself, it was something very natural for him to do. Was this not part of his mission of proclaiming release to captives (Luke 4:18)?

Such, briefly, is the outline of the story or of the story within the story. What, if any, is the connection between us African women theologians and the people in these stories? As a way of establishing this connection, let us look more closely at some salient points of these episodes and ask ourselves a few pertinent questions.

THE STORY OF THE DAUGHTER OF JAIRUS

Luke states that she was "about twelve years" old (8:42). According to Mark, she was squarely "twelve years" old (Mark 5:42). In Jewish society and culture, a girl was understood to have reached her maturity at the age of twelve, while for the boy it was the age of eighteen (cf. Cohen, *Every Man's Talmud*, 162). Jairus' daughter has, therefore, either just attained her maturity or is on the threshold of attaining it. She is thus at a transitional period of her life when she is likely to pass from the authority of her father to that of her husband. Jewish society counseled a father to marry off his daughters at an early age, at twelve and a half. If he did not, his conduct was decried by society.

Whatever the case, Jairus' daughter, who has no name of her own, is projected as a dependent. She is dependent, not only because she is ill and dying, but because as a woman she was expected by society to be dependent. Illness apart, we hear of no action on her part, not till Jesus spoke to her (Luke 8:54). In the sociocultural practice of the time, she would not have been expected to act for herself. Her father was her guardian and spokesman, and soon after it would be her husband. But when Jesus told her, "Child, arise," and directed that she be given something to eat, he was not simply restoring her to life; he was empowering her to take up her life and live. Luke reports that "she got up at once" on her own (8:55), Mark adds that she walked (5:42). Thank God for Jesus!

Now what of us? As African women we, too, are traditionally expected in most of our cultures to be dependent. So far, we, like Jairus' daughter, have largely depended on others to speak for us and present our plight and needs before the world. We have depended either on expatriates (who speak for Africans generally) or on African men to speak for us theologically and otherwise. Has the time now come for us to learn to speak for ourselves? Are we certain that we can and do want to speak for ourselves? Having arisen from the sleep of silence, will we now let others determine how we should speak and do theology? Or will we find our own way of doing theology?

Jairus' daughter is said to have been an only daughter, or, more accurately, an only child. She is, therefore, well beloved by the father who is deeply distressed at the thought of her dying. In a society where men thanked and praised God daily that he had not created them women, and where a blessing prayed God to "bless thee with sons and keep thee from daughters" (Rabbinic interpretation of the blessing of Moses, Num. 6:22–27), it was nevertheless better to have even a female child than to have none at all. So the daughter was precious to her father, and he had to do something to prevent her from dying. Was he concerned merely for himself or was he genuinely concerned for the daughter for her own sake?

We have designated ourselves as the "Circle of Concerned African Women Theologians." I emphasize the word "concerned." What are we concerned about? Whom are we concerned for, ourselves, one another, our people? Why are we concerned? How will we show this concern?

Jesus forbade the parents of the girl to say anything about what he had done. Scholars attribute this to the influence of the Marcan messianic secret motif. But we can say that the living girl was herself testimony enough to the marvel that Jesus had done. Jesus' life-enabling power is best proclaimed by being alive and living. Are we today eloquent testimonies to the marvels that God has worked in our lives? Are we in touch theologically with these marvels? Will we be a theology of praise to our God?

One last word on this story of Jairus' daughter. When Jairus approached Jesus on his knees, Jesus responded directly to him, to his need. But after the worst had happened and common sense had then tried to persuade the father that it would be useless to bother Jesus further, Jesus personally sustained the man's hope: "Do not fear; only believe and she shall be well" (Luke 8:50). He then accompanied him personally to his home and in his very presence and that of the girl's mother, restored the child to life, to their great astonishment. Jesus did more than Jairus had hoped for when he started out to seek his help. Had the daughter already died, he would probably not have set out to seek Jesus' help in the first place (cf. v. 49; John 11:39–40).

Do we, too, go to Jesus on our knees? Are we sure of what kind of help we want from him? Do we believe that he will be able to answer our requests beyond our wildest expectations and dreams? Let us listen to him say to us as he said to Jairus; "Do not fear, only believe and all will be well." We will need to keep our eyes fixed firmly and resolutely on Jesus. We will need, too, to identify and guard against those common sense voices which are likely to tell us not to trouble ourselves or the master, that as Africans and women we are not likely to achieve much. These voices could be our own fears and experiences together, or a feeling that it will not work. They could even be the deeply ingrained but unconscious effects of our customs and taboos. Let us eject from our attitudes and subconscious all prejudices and inferiority complexes about ourselves as Africans and as women. Let us promptly obey Jesus who awakens us from sleep and authorizes and empowers us to undertake responsible theological action and reflection.

THE STORY OF THE WOMAN WITH THE FLOW OF BLOOD

We learn that the woman had suffered from her ailment for "twelve years"; that was the entire life span of Jairus' daughter. Her situation, like that of Jairus' daughter and even more so, was hopeless. Luke says that "she could not be healed by any one" (Luke 8:43). Unlike Mark (5:26), Luke does not add that the woman had "suffered much under many physicians, and had spent all that she had, and was no better, but rather grew worse." Unlike Jairus' daughter, the woman does not seem to have a family or relatives who care. She seems to have been struggling on her own. She may have been either a widow or a woman automatically divorced by virtue of her ailment which automatically rendered her an outcast of society, a permanent source of uncleanness (cf. Lev. 15:25–30).

But the woman had one great asset, namely, her determination to be cured and to take her rightful place in society. It was this determination which led her to brave the crowd and find her own way of touching Jesus. We are not told the cause of her illness; it could not have been of her own making. Merely by being a woman, she was most susceptible to suffering from hemorrhage. But she did not allow herself to be defeated by these natural circumstances. Without her personal determination, she would not have been cured. The desire and the responsibility to be healed lay squarely with her: because she had the will to be healed, she found a way to be healed. Most importantly she found someone to heal her, to affirm her desire to be rid of her infirmity: "Your faith has made you well, go in peace" (Luke 8:48). She became healed, well, "whole," because her courage spoke louder, rose higher, and waxed stronger than the many fears, taboos, prohibitions, and inhibitions traditional in her society, as well as the confirmed hopelessness of her situation. Jesus' remark, "Daughter, your faith has made you well" (Luke 8:48), refers to this determination of hers.

We may compare her with the paralytic of John 5:1–9, who was suffering for thirty-eight years (v. 5), but whom Jesus had to ask whether he "wanted" to be healed (v. 6b). The woman certainly wanted to be healed; she dared to believe, to hope that the impossible could and would happen (so did another Lucan woman, Mary of Nazareth, Luke 1:37–38), and she left no stone unturned to make this happen. In the Lucan perspective, women achieve great things because they dare to believe and trust in the strength of their convictions, that God's power working in them "can do infinitely more than they can ask or imagine" (cf. Eph. 3:20). What was true in Luke's day is still true today since our God is the same yesterday, today and forever.

What do we believe in? Whom do we believe in? Are we determined to give all that it takes to make this happen? Are we convinced that we touch Jesus directly and in one another, and that in our world, all shall be well?

We note, too, that the woman touched Jesus in secret, privately, and had expected it to end there. Her approach was somewhat magic-like. She needed the cure from him (did she consider herself unworthy of such a relationship?). Nor did she want people to know what she had done. But this was not good enough for Jesus. He brought her forward, made her a public figure, called her "daughter," and sent her away in peace.

Obviously, Jesus has done great things for each of us individually, privately; but to show that we have really been healed and freely empowered by God to live, we need to come forward and declare openly, fearlessly, that we have touched and been touched by Jesus, and that this intimate, personal encounter with him has made us "well," that it can also make our whole society well. It is not possible to touch or be touched by Jesus and remain in secret. Once we have really touched him, he will be sure to bring us into the public light, to reassure and praise us for what we have done, for our courage to be, to live.

Peter told Jesus: Everybody is pressing around you, hence, it is only natural that somebody should touch you. We want to touch Jesus by theologizing in our own way, as African women. Why? Is it because everybody else is seeking to do a theology from their own particular perspective: Third World, women, blacks, Latin Americans, Asians, Africans? Or do we want to touch him because we genuinely need wholeness and life from him, both for ourselves individually, for one another and for our people? The woman "felt *in her body* that she was healed of her disease" (Mark 5:29). "Your faith has made you well; go in peace."

The woman was ill for twelve years. Twelve years here may represent the twelve tribes of Israel, the whole of the nation. Her illness has a public, global dimension; it affects society as a whole. Until she is cured, society and the nation cannot be cured. Women need to be restored to their rightful God-given place in society, African society no less than other societies, if the nation and the world are to be made well and are to be brought to marvel at and praise the wonders of God in their midst.

Finally, our entire passage ends or rather continues with Jesus' address to the Twelve. The Twelve are symbolic of the twelve tribes of Israel, the nation (Luke 9:1–2); he calls and endows them with authority and power to go out and preach the Good News, heal in the same way that he had healed both the daughter of Jairus and the woman, enabling the one to "arise" and confirming the other's determination to be cured.

This is the only authentic way of declaring that the "reign of God" has come. For there can be no reign of God where people are considered unclean in society through no sin of theirs, or where no efforts are made to enable them to live fully.

Today, we are not to be satisfied simply with being healed. We are to join the disciples in being healers, in proclaiming that the reign of God has come, that we have touched that reign, become part of it, and have been empowered by God to become its heralds. We are in a unique position to help effect this wholeness of ourselves and of society, because like the woman with the flow of blood we have borne the weight of the illness, the alienation in society, and so should know better where it hurts and how it is to be healed.

The daughter of Jairus and the woman with the flow of blood: two women who met Jesus at a critical point in their lives, when all hope of a cure and restoration was gone, one at the age of twelve, the other after twelve years of illness, one through the intervention of the father, the other by the sheer will to live. Women who were as good as dead, physically and socially, but who were personally touched by Jesus and empowered thereby to arise and live; women who, by living, proclaimed God's marvels and God's Reign. These two women have much to teach us. Let us lend supportive hands to one another and help one another to arise. For Africa will not arise unless its womenfolk, the mothers and bearers of life, arise. What an awesome thought! What a heavy responsibility on our part!

May God give us the will to arise and the desire genuinely to help one another and the whole continent to arise.